Cambridge Elements

Elements in Current Archaeological Tools and Techniques
edited by
Hans Barnard
Cotsen Institute of Archaeology
Willeke Wendrich
Polytechnic University of Turin

DETERMINING PROVENANCE FROM COMPOSITIONAL DATA

Pedro A. López-García
National Institute of Anthropology and History, Mexico

Denisse L. Argote
National Institute of Anthropology and History, Mexico

Shaftesbury Road, Cambridge CB2 8EA, United Kingdom

One Liberty Plaza, 20th Floor, New York, NY 10006, USA

477 Williamstown Road, Port Melbourne, VIC 3207, Australia

314–321, 3rd Floor, Plot 3, Splendor Forum, Jasola District Centre,
New Delhi – 110025, India

Cambridge University Press is part of Cambridge University Press & Assessment,
a department of the University of Cambridge.

We share the University's mission to contribute to society through the pursuit of
education, learning and research at the highest international levels of excellence.

www.cambridge.org
Information on this title: www.cambridge.org/9781009634168
DOI: 10.1017/9781009634205

© Pedro A. López-García and Denisse L. Argote 2026

This publication is in copyright. Subject to statutory exception and to the provisions
of relevant collective licensing agreements, no reproduction of any part may take
place without the written permission of Cambridge University Press & Assessment.

When citing this work, please include a reference to the DOI 10.1017/9781009634205

First published 2026

A catalogue record for this publication is available from the British Library

*A Cataloging-in-Publication data record for this Element is available from the Library
of Congress*

ISBN 978-1-009-63416-8 Hardback
ISBN 978-1-009-63417-5 Paperback
ISSN 2632-7031 (online)
ISSN 2632-7023 (print)

Additional resources for this publication at www.cambridge.org/9781009634168.

Cambridge University Press & Assessment has no responsibility for the persistence
or accuracy of URLs for external or third-party internet websites referred to in this
publication and does not guarantee that any content on such websites is, or will remain,
accurate or appropriate.

For EU product safety concerns, contact us at Calle de José Abascal, 56, 1°, 28003
Madrid, Spain, or email eugpsr@cambridge.org

Determining Provenance from Compositional Data

Elements in Current Archaeological Tools and Techniques

DOI: 10.1017/9781009634205
First published online: February 2026

Pedro A. López-García
National Institute of Anthropology and History, Mexico

Denisse L. Argote
National Institute of Anthropology and History, Mexico

Author for correspondence: Pedro A. López-García, dplopez14@gmail.com

Abstract: Traditionally, classical multivariate statistical methods have been applied to relate cultural materials recovered at archaeological sites to their respective raw material sources. However, when reviewing published research, which usually claims to have reached a high degree of confidence in the assignment of materials, the authors have detected serious errors in the application of these methods, which compromise the inferences made. This Element reconsiders the use of statistical methods in the analysis of the provenance of archaeological materials, using a step-by-step procedure that allows the recognition of natural groups in the data, thus obtaining better-quality classifications while avoiding the problems of total or partial overlaps in the chemical groups (common in biplots). To evaluate the methods proposed here, the challenge of identifying groups in ceramic materials is addressed using algorithms derived from model-based clustering. For cases with partial data labeling, a semi-supervised algorithm is applied to obsidian samples.

Keywords: archaeometry, compositional analysis, model-based clustering, semi-supervised classification, provenance analysis

© Pedro A. López-García and Denisse L. Argote 2026

ISBNs: 9781009634168 (HB), 9781009634175 (PB), 9781009634205 (OC)
ISSNs: 2632-7031 (online), 2632-7023 (print)

Contents

1 Introduction 1

2 Sample Size 5

3 Imputation of Missing Values 6

4 Data Transformation 7

5 Data Diagnosis 11

6 Dimensionality Reduction 12

7 Classification Algorithms 20

8 Model Validation 25

9 Compositional Study of Archaeological Pottery: Example for Variable Selection 28

10 Compositional Study of Obsidian Materials: Example of Semi-Supervised Classification 45

11 Final Comments 55

Appendix: Scripts for R 59

References 68

1 Introduction

Archaeologists have focused on the study of the provenance of cultural materials to solve inquiries such as which natural deposits were exploited in the past, whether the artifacts were of local or foreign origin, what the procedures were for manufacturing specific cultural materials, which routes of exchange existed, and more (Baxter et al., 2003; Glascock, 1992). Nowadays, this kind of research usually includes the use of instrumental analysis techniques, like neutron activation (NAA), X-ray diffraction, and X-ray fluorescence (XRF), among others, basing their inferences mainly on the search for groups with similar physical or chemical characteristics so that cultural questions can be answered. With the advancement of modern technology, archaeologists have access to a greater amount of information. This implies that the data dimensionality is larger and more complex. Therefore, it is necessary to use methods that can process this information to extract the underlying structure of the data.

In the publication *A Systematic Approach to Obsidian Source Characterization* (Glascock et al., 1998), the authors proposed an ordered set of procedures for determining the provenance of obsidian artifacts in which they recommended placing special emphasis on: (i) the collection of samples, (ii) their chemical analysis, and (iii) the statistical procedure. These authors stated that if these steps were properly applied, there could be a high level of confidence in the correct assignment of obsidian artifacts with their respective geological deposits. In the last step, historically, the process of data exploration and classification has been partially solved by using biplots of individual chemical elements or ratios of elements or multivariate statistics such as principal component analysis (PCA), cluster analysis (CA), or discriminant analysis (DA). However, it has now been proved that these classical techniques have serious limitations in terms of their ability to recover the true structure of the cluster or even to recognize that the data do not have real grouping structures. That is why, to validate any type of inference, it takes more than just applying any multivariate technique following pre-established procedures.

By reviewing published literature related to the provenance query, it has become evident that, despite the passage of time, there has been no reflection on the ineffectiveness of the traditional procedures used to associate the samples to their respective natural deposits, which therefore distances the archaeological interpretation from reality due to the propagation of errors introduced by poor data management. For example, we have been able to verify that there are errors in the assignments of samples in many applications. Even in cases in which the original geological sources are known and they belong to different geographical regions, there are overlaps between the groups of samples that make it almost impossible to assign with certainty items to any of the sources or to differentiate sub-sources. These types of results can be the consequence of several factors involved in the handling of the data, among which are an inadequate transformation of the data, an incorrect or absent diagnosis of the results, or a violation in the theoretical assumptions of the classical statistics used, causing the lack of fit between the model and the data and biased results that are far from reality.

In most cases an adequate diagnosis of the data is not made, ignoring the existence of outliers or simply eliminating those samples whose behavior is unusual based on unreliable criteria such as their dispersion according to the standard deviation or their Mahalanobis distance, the latter of which has been proved to have masking and swamping problems that considerably affect it as a reliable criterion for outlier detection (Ben-Gal, 2005). Another example refers to validation, which makes it possible to evaluate the degree of accuracy, bias, reproducibility, success, and traceability of results. When validation is avoided, it is impossible to determine if the studied process or method is suitable for the research, the solution of the algorithm is adequate, and the logic of the procedures to evaluate and validate the results is appropriate. Table 1 summarizes several archaeometric investigations related to provenance studies, indicating where overlap problems are present or what we could consider a lack of fitness or the poor prediction of models.

Nowadays, new, less rigid and more robust clustering and/or classification techniques have been implemented, showing better performance in data handling and allowing more reliable results with a smaller margin of error. However, the procedure for the search of groups is much more complex than has usually been done and involves different steps, all with the sole purpose of being able to give certainty to the inferences made from the data. The order of the steps proposed and described in this Element for processing compositional data acquired from archaeological materials is the following:

1. the selection of the adequate number of samples to be processed;
2. the imputation of values, when few are missing;
3. the choice of the right transformation;
4. the adequate diagnosis of the data using robust methods for outlier detection;
5. the reduction of dimensionality or the selection of variables when dealing with large datasets;
6. the application of clustering algorithms; and
7. the validation of the resulting models.

To exemplify the proposed procedures and the efficiency of variable-selection semi-supervised clustering methods, in Sections 9 and 10, two exercises are described with a practical application to archaeological materials. The scripts

Table 1 Examples of publications that use bivariate plots of elements, ratios between elements, or statistical components and in which overlaps between groups are observed

Reference	Archaeological site and/or geographical region	n	Analytical instrument	Multivariate technique	Bivariate plots	Detected overlaps between sources
Glascock et al., 1998	Central Mexico and Guatemala	712	NAA	PCA	$(\log_{10})$ PC1 vs. PC2	Guatemala region and Orizaba with Otumba; Pachuca 1, 2, and 3
Glascock, 2002	Chichen Itza, Yucatan, Mexico	421	NAA	N/A	Mn vs. Na	Otumba with Paredon
Smith et al., 2007	Yautepec, Morelos, Mexico	390	XRF and NAA	DA	Na vs. Mn; Dy vs. Nm	Otumba with Paredon; Fuentezuelas with El Paraiso
Glascock et al., 2010	Western and Central Mexico	596	long and short NAA, and XRF	N/A	Cs and Sc; Mn vs. Na; Mn vs. Dy	Ucareo with Altotonga; Ucareo with Zinapecuaro; Sta. Elena with Paredon, Otumba, Malpaís, and Derrumbadas; Zaragoza with Altotonga; Sierra Pachca 2 with Tulancingo; Sierra Pachca 3 with Pengamo 1, 2, and Fuentezuelas; Altotonga with Ucareo
Glascock et al., 2010	Jalisco, Nayarit, and Zacatecas, Mexico	>1,000	XRF	N/A	Rb vs. Zr	Overlapping between several deposits from Nayarit (San Lionel, Ixtlan del Rio), Zacatecas (Huistla) and Jalisco (Llano Grande, San Isidro, Hacienda Guadalupe, La Lobera, Ixtepete, Sta.

Table 1 (cont.)

Reference	Archaeological site and/or geographical region	n	Analytical instrument	Multivariate technique	Bivariate plots	Detected overlaps between sources
Millhauser et al., 2011	Xaltocan, Tlaxcalla, Mexico	103	pXRF	PCA and CA	PC1 vs. PC2	Teresa, La Providencia, Osotero, San Juan de los Arcos, Boquillas, Navaja, Ahisculco, and La Quemada) Otumba with Paredon; Tulancingo and Tepalzingo with Penjamo; Cruz Negra with Zinapecuaro and Ucareo; Magdalena with Tequila and Ixtepeque; Derrumbadas with El Chayal
Moholy-Nagy et al., 2013	Tikal, Guatemala	2,283	pXRF	N/A	Ir vs. Mg; Rb vs. Zr	Ixtepeque with Otumba and Paredon; Cerro Varal with Ucareo and San Martin Jilotepeque
Pierce, 2015	Western Mexico	>1,000	XRF	N/A	Fe vs. Mn	All West Mexican sources
Waite, 2020	Coba, Quintana Roo, and Yucatan	113	pXRF	N/A	Sr vs. Zr; Rb vs. Zr; Zr vs. Sr	Ixtepeque with Otumba; Zacualtipan with Zaragoza and Ucareo

Note: NAA = neutron activation analysis; PCA = principal component analysis; N/A = no multivariate analysis was applied (only biplots); PC1 = first principal component; PC2 = second principal component; XRF = X ray fluorescence; pXRF = portable X ray fluorescence.

related to each step of the process, which should be run in the open-source R environment (R Core Team, 2020), are provided in the Appendix.

2 Sample Size

The provenance postulate explicitly states that in order to determine the sources of origin of archaeological artifacts through compositional analysis, samples extracted from the same deposit of raw material must register a lower chemical variability than the variability observed between different sources of raw material (Weigand et al., 1977). Therefore, when studying a deposit, the internal variability of the site must be considered, as well as how homogeneous its composition is, understanding "variability" as the measure of the dispersion of data in a distribution, whether theoretical or of a sample (Dagnino, 2014). For example, if in a volcanic region there were various eruptive events that caused the formation of sub-sources, it would be necessary to study the variability of each of these and, simultaneously, assess the variability between the deposits of the different regions. Theoretically, the distribution of each particular source or sub-source should be different, and this should be reflected in the chemical variability of its components. It should be noted that variability in the data may also come from measurement errors of the studied features.

A sample is a significant fraction of the total population. So, to obtain consistent statistical results, the sample size is critical in any inferential study. Statistically speaking, if the number of observations (n) becomes larger, the type I error decreases and, therefore, the precision error too. In addition, in techniques that assume normality of the data, the central limit theorem becomes operational. Thus, to estimate variability, it is necessary to consider a statistically adequate sample size so that the estimates are unbiased, and it is advisable that this be at least $n \geq 30$. Some authors, like Glascock et al. (1998), recommend that a sample of at least 12 units of analysis be taken in order to determine the range of variation in the composition of simple obsidian deposits and at least 100 units of analysis in cases where the deposits are more extensive and complex (Glascock et al., 1998). Ben Dor et al. (2023), by evaluating several statistical techniques, proposed that 10 to 20 specimens are enough for distinguishing sources with a certainty of >0.9, depending on the inherent variability of the studied materials. However, regardless of the sample size, the higher the n (i.e., $n \to \infty$), the more statistically accurate the estimation of the parameters will be, and the fewer biases will be involved.

For example, Cobean (2002) presented the results of the NAA analysis of samples from 20 obsidian deposits in central Mexico, publishing only descriptive statistics such as mean, standard deviation, and minimum and maximum values. Although for 14 of these sources he was able to analyze 30 samples, for six sources he analyzed much fewer: in the case of Derrumbadas, in Puebla, only five ($n = 5$) samples were analyzed; for Tepalzingo, in Hidalgo, $n = 10$; for Pachuca 2, in Hidalgo, $n = 11$; for Cruz Negra, in Michoacán, $n = 15$; for Penjamo 1, in Guanajuato, $n = 12$; and for Penjamo 2, $n = 15$. In cases where $n < 30$, nothing can be generalized when measuring variables that have variation in the population, so it is necessary to increase the sample size to have a better idea of the variability of these deposits. On the other hand, for these same cases, descriptive statistics and punctual estimators such as mean and standard deviation, among others, are not sufficient to estimate the unknown parameters of the population, so the estimates can be biased. For these reasons, you cannot have complete confidence in the results obtained with small sample sizes.

3 Imputation of Missing Values

It is common to come across the problem of recording missing data or data that are below the limit of detection (LOD). To elude this problem, a common approach is to remove variables with zeros, negative values, or missing values. This approach is considered an aggressive method of elimination or, in the words of Michael Baxter and Hilary Cool (2016), a draconian approach, since the removal of an entire variable means some existing data are also deleted, leading to a significant loss of information. Instead, to avoid significant data loss, we recommend using value substitution, also called imputation. In the case of compositional data where one or more components may have the problem of being below the LOD, multiple imputations can be used to produce a single value that will be used to replace the missing data, reducing bias in the estimates.

In some cases, missing values have been substituted using the Mahalanobis distance, but this distance is not an imputation method since it only minimizes the distance of the missing data from the centroid of the dataset (Glascock, 2011). Imputation methods such as Mahalanobis distance can distort the covariance structure of the data and, in general, the covariance structure of the parties involved (Martín-Fernández et al., 2003). In this Element, we recommend the use of two packages written for the R environment for the imputation of values: multivariate imputation by chained equations (**MICE**) (van Buuren & Groothuis-Oudshoorn, 2011) and **zCompositions** (Palarea-Albaladejo & Martín-Fernández, 2015). The former is recommended for missing or zero values, while the latter is useful for values that are below the LOD of the instrument.

Multivariate imputation by chained equations is used to impute multiple replacement values for missing multivariate data. This method specifies the multivariate imputation model on a variable-by-variable basis using a set of conditional densities, one for each incomplete variable. Starting from an initial value, **MICE** obtains imputations by iterating on conditional densities, so it is recommended for cases where an adequate multivariate distribution of the data cannot be found. To inspect the distributions of the original and imputed data, **MICE** has the "stripplot()" function; the graphs show the distribution of the variables as individual points. The full data values are recorded in blue, while the imputed values are shown in red. The imputed values should suitably follow the pattern of the non-imputed values.

For its part, zCompositions is a package that runs under the compositional approach for the imputation of left-censored data, or data < LOD. Its 'log-ratio DA' algorithm is available, which imputes values < LOD through simulated values of their posterior predictive distributions through the representation of coordinates that take as a reference the values recorded from the rest of the data. In addition, it uses an iterative Markov chain Monte Carlo procedure that is incorporated as a maximum likelihood method with the expectation maximization (EM) algorithm to estimate the parameters of the common conjugate normal-inverse-Wishart probability distribution with non-informative Jeffreys prior. The method gives special relevance to aspects related to compositional data, such as scale invariance, sub-compositional coherence, and the preservation of the multivariate relative structure of the data.

4 Data Transformation

Once compositional data (expressed in weight percentages or parts per million) have been acquired from the archaeological materials employing the preferred analytical technique, it must be decided whether it is necessary to transform them or not. It is important to note that the type of transformation employed has a lot to do with the results obtained, since many techniques are based on the calculation of measurements of dissimilarity of Euclidean distance that are dependent on the scale; similarly, other techniques rely on theoretical assumptions such as the normality of the data or the homogeneity of variance of the groups – conditions that are not always fulfilled. Although on certain occasions the assumption of multivariate normality is not a requirement, as is the case with exploratory analyses such as PCA, CA, or partial least squares, if the behavior of the data is close to normal, the results of exploratory analyses will show more evident separations between the groups of data.

In the published literature, there are those who analyze the raw data (Ambrose et al., 2009; Dolan, 2016; Glascock, 2002), those who argue in favor of standardizing the data to the Z-score with mean zero and variance 1 (Baxter, 2001; Baxter, 2015; Baxter & Buck, 2000), those who transform data to $\log_{10}$ (Glascock et al., 1998; Hall, 2004; Hall & Minyaev, 2002; Millhauser et al., 2011), and those who recommend log ratio transformations (Aitchison, 1986; Greenacre, 2017; Martín-Fernández et al., 2015). However, raw data can have substantial differences of magnitude, and the variables can have different types of distributions. Considering that many multivariate techniques use distance calculation to detect patterns in the data, it is obvious that the magnitude of the differences between the variables will have an impact on the calculation of the differences between the variables. That is, if the data are processed as they were measured, the variables with a greater range of variation or greater variance will have a greater influence on the modeling, and the variables that could have some type of structure will be difficult to detect.

In contrast, if the data are measured on different measurement scales, they cannot be compared, so it is necessary to make sure all the variables have the same scale so that they can be compared. That is why Baxter and Buck (2000) recommend the standardization of archaeometric data with simple Z-score normalization, which is equivalent to a linear transformation, calculated by

$$z = \frac{x - \bar{x}}{\sigma_x}. \tag{1}$$

where x is the original value of the variable, $\bar{x}$ is the mean of the variable, and σ_x is the standard deviation. The authors argue that the values obtained through this transformation make up variables with the same weight; in this way, the components will have a distribution that is closer to normal. However, standardization is only recommended to eliminate dependence on the units of measurement used, that is, when the variables have different units of measurement and very different ranges (Wehrens, 2011). Moreover, this transformation is not enough to modify more complex features of a distribution such as asymmetry, so nonlinear transformations must be made instead. In this regard, Reimann et al. (2002) stated that Z standardization makes little sense in geochemistry since it is known that the empirical distributions of the data are strongly biased.

In the research conducted by Milligan & Cooper (1988) with eight different methods of standardization under several error conditions (including error-free data, error-perturbed distances, the inclusion of outliers, and the addition of random noise dimensions), it was shown that, for variables measured in the same units, standardization of the Z-score is not advisable as it can remove important information about the variation between groups. In addition, standardization is less sensitive to observations at the boundaries between groups and to the existence of outliers. The authors' experiments also showed that those approaches that standardize using the division by rank of the variable (i.e., the difference between the maximum and minimum value) yield a consistently superior retrieval of the group structure. Furthermore, when standardized data are clustered using conventional clustering techniques, outliers are usually forced to merge with existing clusters in the data (Milligan & Cooper, 1988).

The conversion of data to $\log_{10}$ is another very commonly applied transformation, whose use is assumed to prevent some variables from having a greater weight and playing a dominant role in the classification. In the case of trace elements, the trend of the data gets closer to normal (Glascock, 1992; Neff, 1992). Nonetheless, Reimann et al. (2002) proved that most geochemical datasets do not show behavior approaching normal or logarithmic normal and that even when other transformation methods are used with $\log_{10}$, more than 70% of all components in each dataset do not approximate normal distribution. This is because data of this nature present problems of multimodality and the presence of outliers. Baxter & Cool (2016) have also shown that geochemical data tend to have longer tails than would be expected for normally distributed data and that the transformation $\log_{10}$ does not avoid the dominant effects of greater variance in some of the variables. In personal experiments made with databases of both lithic and ceramic analyzed with NAA and pXRF, in which we transformed chemical data to $\log_{10}$ and used histograms and normal probability graphs to assess whether there was any deviation from normal, we verified that this transformation did not yield normality in most cases.

For any analysis, it is important to first consider the intrinsic nature of the data. It is undeniable that compositional data are vectors of strictly positive data and that the range of values they can take varies from 0 to k, where k is a constant ($k = 1$, 100%, or 10^6 parts per million [ppm]). These restrictions cause the compositional data to follow another geometry, called Aitchison geometry (Aitchison, 1986). In this, the geometric space is called the simplex, and any vector x, whose components are D-parts of a whole, is subject to the constraint that the sum of its parts must be equal to the constant k, so it is a closed space. In this way, the simplex allows compositions to be represented in orthogonal coordinates. Recognizing the properties of compositional data, in this Element we recommend using the Aitchison method, which is based on the transfer of compositional data from the restricted space to the multivariate real space based on the logarithms of the ratios between the parts (Mateu-Figueras et al., 2003). These transformations include the additive log ratio, the centered log ratio (*clr*), and the isometric log ratio (*ilr*) (Pawlowsky-Glahn & Buccianti,

2011). With these transformations, the condition of the constant sum is fulfilled, leading to data that are not constrained and that can take any real value between $-\infty$ and $+\infty$. Working with log ratios also ensures a basic logical principle of sub-compositional coherence (Mateu-Figueras et al., 2003).

Once this transformation is made, the data can be analyzed using any multivariate analysis technique (Aitchison, 2003; Pawlowsky-Glahn & Egozcue, 2006; Pawlowsky-Glahn et al., 2007). To effectively conduct the procedures described here, in this Element it was decided to work with the *clr* and *ilr* transformations. The *clr* transformation uses the geometric mean of the sample vector as a reference and has a one-to-one relationship between the original *D*-parts. The *ilr* coordinates map a composition in the *D*-part Aitchison's simplex, isometrically turning it into a *D*-1 dimensional Euclidean vector (Egozcue et al., 2003; Filzmoser et al., 2009). In this way, an orthonormal base can be defined with each element of the simplex identified according to its coordinate vector, allowing the direct handling of the geometric elements in this space (Egozcue et al., 2003). The advantage of these transformations is that they preserve all the metric properties of the compositional data, such as isometry and the non-singular covariance matrix (Egozcue & Pawlowsky-Glahn, 2011).

It is important to emphasize that, although compositional data are presented as weight percentages, proportions, or ppm, the sum of each of the vectors rarely adds up to the constant k. Strictly speaking, such data are always sub-compositions, since only a subset of the components is measured or recorded. This means that there is an additional implicitly defined component, known as the residual part, which completes the constant k (Pawlowsky-Glahn & Egozcue, 2006). In order to respect the constant sum constraint, there are two options: either you can add the residual variable or you can close the data. In the first option, the residual variable is calculated by summing each of the parts of the vector and subtracting them from the constant k (given in percentages or ppm); the difference will make up the residual variable (Baxter et al., 2003; Baxter et al., 2005). For the second case, the vector can be normalized with the closure operator:

$$(x) = \left[\frac{k \cdot x_1}{\sum_{i=1}^{D} x_i}, \frac{k \cdot x_2}{\sum_{i=1}^{D} x_i}, \ldots, \frac{k \cdot x_D}{\sum_{i=1}^{D} x_i} \right]. \qquad (2)$$

This transforms each vector of *D*-parts so that its components sum to a constant k (Baxter et al., 2005; Egozcue & Pawlowsky-Glahn, 2011). The components of the closed vector are called parts and constitute the simplex of *D*-parts. Either of these two operations yields completely compositional data, which can then be transformed into log ratio coordinates. To transform the data to the centered and/or the isometric log ratio, the "compositions" package for R can be used (van den Boogaart et al., 2023).

5 Data Diagnosis

Another important point to consider is the proper diagnosis of the data, as it has been shown that the presence of outliers can have a strong impact on estimates (Filzmoser et al., 2012; Hubert & Van der Veeken, 2008). Outliers are experimental units that present a value or combination of values in the recorded variables that clearly differentiate them from the rest of the observations; in other words, an outlier is an observation that deviates considerably from the other observations in the sample set (Hawkins, 1980; van den Boogaart & Tolosana-Delgado, 2013). Nowadays, it is recommended to use robust methods that have greater resistance to the presence of outliers and that exceed the performance of classic statistics. For example, Mahalanobis distance presents two types of classification error that occur in the presence of outliers within the data: the "masking" of an outlier as a non-outlier and the "swamping" of a non-outlier as an outlier. For this reason, it is important to detect outliers so that the soundness of the procedures can be rigorously evaluated.

Given the high-dimensional nature of compositional data, the use of multivariate approaches for outlier detection is recommended, like the robust PCA method called "ROBPCA" (Hubert et al., 2005). This method reduces the dimensionality of data: the robust loadings are computed by applying projection-pursuit techniques, and the minimum covariance determinant method is used to determine the robust center and covariance matrix. The ROBPCA algorithm produces a diagnostic plot that shows and classifies outliers. However, this algorithm runs under the assumption that regular observations are normally distributed. Therefore, given the asymmetric nature of compositional data, it is recommended to use an alternative algorithm, known as skewness-adjusted outlyingness (Hubert & Van der Veeken, 2008).

Adjusted outlyingness is a generalization of Stahel–Donoho outlyingness, which does not need the assumption of normality to be fulfilled and is not based on visual inspection. This estimator detects outliers in multivariate biased data based on the outer limit of the data points with respect to the data core; outliers are essentially obtained by projecting observations in many univariate directions and calculating a robust center and scale at each projection. When the sample size (n) is large enough compared to the dimension p, the number of components ($n > 5*p$) generates orthogonal directions to the hyperplane through p random observations, so the adjusted outlyingness will then be affine invariant (Hubert & Van der Veeken, 2008).

To find outliers with the adjusted outlyingness (AO) algorithm, we recommend employing the function "adjOutlyingness" of the package **robustbase** (Maechler, 2023). In the process, the AO algorithm computes the "medcouple" – a robust concept and estimator of skewness. The medcouple is defined as a scaled median difference between the left and right half of a distribution, and hence is not based on the third moment, as in classical skewness. The observations are then weighted according to their outliers, and robust Stahel–Donoho estimates are obtained with a weighted mean and a covariance matrix. An observation is labeled as atypical when its adjusted outlyingness is too great (Hubert & Van der Veeken, 2008).

6 Dimensionality Reduction

In the current published literature, it has been shown that not all variables are relevant in the task of clustering and that many of them make up noise, providing little or no information and having a negative impact on the detection of the underlying structure of the data and especially on the estimation of the optimal number of groups (Scrucca & Raftery, 2018). Thus, considering all variables simultaneously in an analysis or taking only a subset without considering a statistically sound procedure can have negative effects on the pooling results (Andrews & McNicholas, 2014; Fop & Murphy, 2018; Scrucca & Raftery, 2018). In provenance studies we can find three different approaches concerning the inclusion or exclusion of variables, which are described in Sections 6.1, 6.2, and 6.3.

6.1 First Approach: Subjective Approach

The first approach, which we call the subjective approach, is one in which it is stated that certain components are more effective than others in discriminating compositional groups based on personal opinions (Craig et al., 2007; Glascock et al., 2010; Mendelsohn, 2018; Moholy-Nagy et al., 2013). In this approach, the criteria for arriving at such statements are not discussed in detail, although the most common tactic is to display two of the components or ratios between components in bivariate graphs (Iñañez et al., 2009; Italiano et al., 2018; Tykot, 2016; Waite, 2020). The first thing to note here is that the use of bivariate plots turns out to be a subjective procedure, since choosing which pair of variables offers the best separation consists of examining a total of $p!/2!(p-2)!$ graphics, making it impractical when you have a large number of variables (Salem & Hussein, 2019). For example, if we obtained $p = 28$ components when analyzing our samples with NAA, a total of 378 bivariate plots would have to be inspected to select the one that we thought better fit our hypotheses.

In most of the published cases, a great deal of overlap is observed between the points that make up the assumed groups. In other cases, a dissimilarity in the number of identified groups can be seen depending on which components are graphed. In Table 1, there are detailed examples of publications that use bivariate graphs of elements, ratios between elements, or statistical components (i.e., PCA), showing the overlapping of their groups. However, some of the minor and trace elements vary considerably in concentration from one instrument to another due to the different detection limits and working ranges managed by each. The calibrations and standards used also vary from technique to technique, which can cause the concentrations of elements and accuracy of results to be different in data recorded with different instruments. Therefore, this approach is not recommended.

6.2 Second Approach: Feature Extraction

The second approach, known as feature extraction, states that the inclusion of the largest possible number of components in the analysis is preferable to achieve effective discrimination of chemical groups. The inclusion of all the components (or as many as possible) is due to the idea that, if only a limited number of components are analyzed, it will not be possible to obtain an optimal result since it is unknown a priori which of the components will be most effective for the discrimination of the groups (Glascock, 2011; Harbottle, 1976). In this approach, the most common dimensionality reduction methods aim to apply linear transformations to project the data onto a subspace derived from the original space; examples of these methods are PCA and linear DA (LDA). Principal component analysis bases its estimates on the mean vectors and the covariance matrix, replacing the original data matrix with a coordinate system in which variance is maximized (Thrun, 2018) and where it is established that the greatest amount of information (the greatest variability or variance captured) is contained in the fewest possible components.

The percentage of cumulative variance explained by the components is considered a measure of the quality of the projection, thus reflecting the situation of the experimental units in the high-dimensional space (Varmuza & Filzmoser, 2009). It is important to consider that PCA analysis assumes that the variables are highly correlated; however, if the correlation is not linear, the characteristics that differentiate the groups will not be orthogonal, and the principal components (PCs) cannot be adequately determined. There are databases in which groups are difficult to discriminate or at least are not linearly separable; examples of this are the data from Chainlink (Ultsch, 1995), on leukemia (Haferlach et al., 2010), and on iris flowers (Fisher, 1936). Of these, the best-known database in the pattern recognition literature is that of iris flowers, whose dataset has three classes (*Iris setosa*, *Iris versicolor*, and *Iris virginica*) with 50 instances each, of which four morphological characteristics were measured. Using unsupervised exploratory techniques, only two of the groups could be discriminated, while the third group was more difficult to separate; moreover, the groups were not separable without the information from the labels of each flower.

For this reason, it is very important to consider which dimensionality reduction method(s) to use, since, if the data have a certain tendency and do not fit the model, certain projection techniques can introduce spurious groups. In archaeology, it is very common to find publications that use PCA or LDA for the reduction of dimensionality and data processing (Glascock et al., 1998; Millhauser et al., 2011; Smith et al., 2007), both of which have their pros and cons. In this regard, PCA is sensitive to the scale of measurement of characteristics. That is why standardization with mean 0 and variance 1 should only be applied in cases where the scale of measurement of the variables is recorded in different types of units, otherwise the variables whose scale is larger will dominate and therefore contribute more to the overall variance. It should be remembered that PCA is not robust against outliers, since their significant presence will bias the classic matrices of location and dispersion. This is one of the reasons why it is recommended to perform a good diagnosis of the data using robust methods to detect or remove outliers before performing PCA or any other multivariate technique.

In addition to the above, PCA has other limitations. For example, PCA assumes that the compositional dataset has no missing values (no empty rows), so the imputation of the missing values must be ensured using a robust method. Only if the missing values are a higher percentage within a variable is it advisable to remove the whole component. Another limitation is the assumption of orthogonality of the PCs, since they are by design orthogonal to each other. Depending on the situation, there may be more "appropriate" base vectors to reduce data that are not orthogonal. Another drawback is that, as a projection method, PCA uses the plane of the two major axes of the ellipsoid; in this regard, it has been shown that the visualization of structures in high-dimensional data based on plane projections is difficult to interpret and favors overlap between groups, causing the partition of data points that belong to the same group into several different groups (Ultsch & Thrun, 2017).

Conversely, LDA is used to find a linear combination of features that characterizes or separates two or more classes. Being a supervised classifier, the labels in the learning samples are assumed to be error-free. This causes LDA to be sensitive to noise, so if the learning dataset contains some wrong labels, biased results can be obtained (Bouveyron et al., 2019). Another limitation of this technique derives from two of its essential theoretical assumptions: (1) the distribution of input variables must follow a Gaussian distribution, and (2) the variances between groups must be homogeneous. Finally, LDA is also extremely sensitive to outliers, and in cases where the number of observations exceeds the number of features, LDA may not work well. All the above results in LDA not being suitable for nonlinear problems and not performing well for unbalanced datasets.

6.3 Third Approach: Feature or Variable Selection

The third approach is related to finding the most informative components that can contribute to the clustering or classification, which can be a challenge in cases such as archaeometry. This step is important because when a learning model has a greater number of components, it tends to overadjust and its performance loses predictive power (Alelyani et al., 2014). In addition, the inclusion of redundant components in the model introduces noise, which leads to the fact that the true structure of data clustering is not discovered (Xie, Pan & Shen, 2008). It has been shown that non-informative variables, or "masking variables" (Fowlkes & Mallows, 1983), can cause errors in the grouping results (Wang & Zhu, 2008). Conversely, it has been shown that selecting an optimal subset of features can facilitate both model fitting and interpretation of results (Andrews & McNicholas, 2014; Raftery & Dean, 2006).

Feature selection is the process of choosing a smaller subset of features that preserves only the most important and/or relevant variables in the dataset according to a certain evaluation criterion (Alelyani et al., 2014). A variable is considered relevant if it is useful for discovering groups or classes; otherwise, it is irrelevant. On the other hand, a variable is considered redundant if it is highly correlated with other variables. In real life, any high-dimensional database will have variables relevant for discriminating groups and will also contain variables whose information is not meaningful, therefore causing the accuracy of the grouping to be negatively affected if all of them are used. Using all available variables will increase the complexity of the model and decrease the performance of the classification method; but selecting the best set of features that substantially contribute to the tasks of data analysis can achieve higher performance in the classification. Based on this fact, different clustering techniques have been proposed that use variable selection methods, like the ones we will see later in this Element.

Baxter and Jackson (2001) pointed out that the operation of variable selection is inevitable in archaeometric work, proposing two methods to reduce dimensionality and be able to retain only the informative variables based on the analysis of PCs and classification trees; but, for the reasons already explained, these methods proved to be ineffective. In most cases in archaeometry, the selection of variables to discriminate groups has been made arbitrarily and without theoretical foundations, arguing that a few bivariate graphs are enough to relate the samples to their respective sites (Baxter et al., 2003; Glascock, 2011). It should be borne in mind that, in each study, the properties of the materials are different; therefore, it cannot be generalized. If, in the classification of certain material, the selection of certain variables obtained a good result, it is not equivalent to affirming that comparable results can be obtained in all studies on this subject. In other words, there is no guarantee that selecting the same variables for two different studies will yield similar results.

The above can be clearly examined in published references, in which overlaps in the data or variation in the number of groups can commonly be seen when trying to classify ceramic and lithic materials using combinations of elements in bivariate graphs. Personally, we believe that looking for the fastest solution in the provenance analysis does not always have optimal results. Considering that our approach is based on the analysis of log ratios with strictly positive D-components, the selection of compositional data variables can be done in two different ways: selecting parts or selecting log ratios. If you choose to work with parts, you must find a subset of them based on an optimization criterion, then close the data and process it with log ratios using this sub-composition. If you prefer to work directly with log ratios, a subset of the transformed parts will be selected using a statistical criterion for further analysis (Greenacre, 2017). For example, Ben Dor et al. (2023) applied an approach based on the *clr* transformation and considering the *p*-value of the Kruskal–Wallis test and their pairwise correlation structure.

Although there are a large number of published methods for feature selection (filters, wrappers, and hybrid models), our goal is not to provide an exhaustive comparison of variable selection methods; such comparisons can be found in other references (Maugis et al., 2009a, 2009b; Raftery & Dean, 2006; Scrucca & Raftery, 2018). Our aim in any case is to show that proper preprocessing of data along with variable selection increases both model performance and interpretation. However, an adequate definition of the basic concepts must be made, particularly exploring parametric methods for variable selection with finite mixture model-based clustering (MBC).

Model-based clustering places the clustering task in a formal modeling framework where the empirical distribution of data is modeled through a finite mixture of theoretical probability distributions, typically the multivariate Gaussian distribution (Fop & Murphy, 2018). Here, each component

k (group) is modeled using the Gaussian distribution, whose parameters are represented by μ_k (vector of means) and Σk (covariance matrix). Therefore, discovering the optimal number of groups and the best cluster model will be a statistical model selection problem in which there is a finite number of candidate models with different numbers and types of component distributions (Fraley & Raftery, 1998). In this sense, it is considered that the data come from different groups or subpopulations that correspond to the components of the mixture. Thus, by assuming that the experimental data in the different groups were generated by different probability distributions, reference is made to the provenance postulate (Weigand et al., 1977), which establishes that different chemical groups represent different sources that are discriminated due to their particular internal compositional variability.

Variable selection methods point out that it is essential to distinguish between relevant and irrelevant variables (Fop & Murphy, 2018). Relevant variables are defined in terms of statements of probabilistic dependence (or independence); these hold the purest and most contamination-free information and turn out to be fundamental in the grouping. On the other hand, irrelevant variables, as their name implies, are unimportant and are divided into redundant and non-informative variables. The former are called "redundant" because in other variables you already have the information you need; that is, they are strongly correlated and can be omitted without incurring much loss of information. The latter are variables that do not contribute to the model since they correspond to noise, so they lack information. Variable selection and MBC consider these distribution assumptions on the relevant and irrelevant variables.

The advantage of using these methods is that, instead of obtaining a single output or result such as a dendrogram or a two-dimensional projection (i.e., PCA or LDA), MBC uses the same matrix of input data to obtain m candidate models, which are compared to each other using a model selection criterion (Fop & Murphy, 2018). Once the best model has been chosen within this finite family of models, simultaneously, the most relevant variables for clustering and the optimal number of clusters are automatically selected by the algorithm, retaining in the end the cluster model that best fits the empirical data (Celeux & Govaert, 1995).

In the mathematical context, by assuming that the sample components are extracted from a multivariate normal mixture, a model $f(\bullet|\theta_k)MVN(\bullet|\mu_k, \Sigma_k)$ is obtained where $\theta_k = (\pi_1, \ldots, \pi_{k-1})$ are the mixing probabilities such that $\theta_k \geq 0$ and $\Sigma \theta_k = 1$, and $MNV(\bullet|\mu_k, \Sigma_k)$ is the q-dimensional Gaussian density function with parameters μ_k (which corresponds to the vector of means) and Σ_k (which is the matrix of covariances). The mixture is characterized by the constraints imposed on the Σ_k matrices in terms of their eigenvalue decomposition, which allows the generation of different geometric properties of the candidate models that are obtained through the Gaussian components. These constraints are summarized in the three terms to the right of Equation (3),

$$\Sigma_k = \lambda_k D_k A_k D'_k, \tag{3}$$

where the first term (λ_k) indicates the constraints on the volume parameter in the kth cluster, the second term (D_k) indicates the constraints on the orientation of the groups in the matrix, and the third term (A_k) indicates the constraints on the array of the group shapes.

In the context of MBC, the R package **clustvarsel** version ≥2.0 (Scrucca & Raftery, 2018) performs the selection of subsets of informative variables based on a wrapper method. This package runs in conjunction with the **mclust** package (Fraley et al., 2012), which allows automatic selection of the number of components in the mixture together with the selection of covariance structures from the parameterization of eigenvalue decomposition (see Eq. 3). With **mclust**, you can specify $m = 14$ potential models with different geometric features. Raftery and Dean (2006) propose dividing X variables in the model into three sets that have no elements in common:

1. X^C = the set of current clustering variables;
2. X^P = the variable(s) proposed for inclusion or exclusion from the set of clustering variables;
3. X^{NC} = the set of other variables not significant for clustering.

According to Raftery and Dean (2006), the solution to the problem of variable selection is based on the use of the Bayesian information criterion (BIC) to approximate Bayes factors to compare adjusted mixed models in nested subsets of variables (Scrucca & Raftery, 2018). That is, the candidate models are compared using the BIC approximation to their marginal probabilities:

$$\text{BIC}_A = \text{BIC}_{\text{clust}}(\mathbf{X}^C, \mathbf{X}^P), \tag{4}$$

$$\text{BIC}_B = \text{BIC}_{\text{no clust}}(\mathbf{X}^C) + \text{BIC}_{\text{reg}}(\mathbf{X}^P|\mathbf{X}^C), \tag{5}$$

where $\text{BIC}_{\text{clust}}(\mathbf{X}^C, \mathbf{X}^P)$ is the BIC of a Gaussian mixture model in which $\mathbf{X}^P$ adds relevant information for clustering, $\text{BIC}_{\text{no clust}}(\mathbf{X}^C)$ is the BIC of the MBC on the current set of clustering variables, and $\text{BIC}_{\text{reg}}(\mathbf{X}^P|\mathbf{X}^C)$ is the BIC of the regression of $\mathbf{X}^P$ on $\mathbf{X}^C$. If the difference $\text{BIC}_A - \text{BIC}_B$ is > 0, $\mathbf{X}^P$ is included in the clustering variable set. To make the selection, variables are added/removed, and different models are compared using a stepwise greedy search algorithm (Fop & Murphy, 2018).

The R package **SelvarMix** version 1.0 (Sedki et al., 2014, 2017) provides a method based on the approach described by Maugis et al. (2009b), preceded by a step in which the variables are ranked using a regularization of the likelihood procedure (ℓ_1), which is a procedure for selecting and estimating linear models. The ℓ_1 penalty is placed on the Gaussian mixture mean vectors and the Gaussian mixture component precision matrices (Sedki et al., 2014). This model, called SRUW, distinguishes between relevant variables (*S*) and irrelevant variables (*Sc*), dividing the latter into two classes. A part (U) of the irrelevant variables may depend on a subset (R) of the relevant variables, and another part (W) is independent of other variables. The parameters of the mixture are estimated by maximum likelihood using the EM algorithm (Dempster et al., 1977), and both the number of *K* components and the shape of the mixture are chosen using the BIC.

The SRUW model reformulates the variable selection problem for MBC as a model selection problem (Maugis et al., 2009b), where candidate models are indexed by maximizing a BIC-type criterion:

$$\text{crit}(K, m, r, \ell, V) = \text{BIC}_{\text{clust}}(y^S | K, m) + \text{BIC}_{\text{reg}}(y^U | r, y^R) + \text{BIC}_{\text{indep}}(y^W | \ell), \quad (6)$$

where $\text{BIC}_{\text{clust}}$ is the BIC criterion of the MBC of the relevant variables (S), BIC_{reg} represents the BIC criterion of the regression model of the irrelevant variables (U) on the subset of relevant variables (R), and $\text{BIC}_{\text{indep}}$ represents the BIC criterion of the Gaussian model with the variables (W) independent of the other variables (Sedki, Celeux & Maugis, 2014).

Finally, the **VarSelLCM** variable selection method (Marbac & Sedki, 2017) allows the complete selection of the model and the selection of variables, in addition to the optimal number of clusters. The procedure rests on the assumption of conditional independence and on a new information criterion based on the integrated complete-data likelihood, named the maximum integrated complete-data likelihood criterion, which does not require multiple calls of the EM algorithm. In this, a variable is not significant for clustering if its one-dimensional marginal distributions are equal between classes. To recognize that a variable is relevant, the authors introduce a binary indicator variable $\omega = (\omega_1, \ldots, \omega_j, \ldots, \omega_J)$, such that $\omega_j = 1$ if the variable X_j is relevant; otherwise, $\omega_j = 0$. In this way, candidate models are defined both by the number of components and by the vector ω. These methods can be used to select the variables relevant to MBC in Gaussian mixture configurations.

7 Classification Algorithms

Another important aspect is to carefully consider the algorithm(s) for the clustering and/or classification task, whose main goal is to partition the total set of data into subsets (called clusters) whose characteristics are similar; that is, to uncover meaningful groups in data based on the principle of maximizing intra-class similarity and minimizing inter-class similarity (Heller, 2007). According to the type of groups obtained, clustering algorithms can be classified as disjoint or fuzzy (Jain & Dubes, 1988). In the first, also known as hard (crisp) partitioning techniques, each experimental unit is assigned to one, and only one, compact cluster with well-defined boundaries that is well separated from the other clusters. It is assumed that the samples in a group are more like each other because they share common characteristics referring to their class, which allows a relationship of similarity and uniformity to be established between them. In contrast, in fuzzy sets, data boundaries are not defined, and sample items may belong to more than one of the clusters into which the dataset has been divided, but with a certain value or degree of membership (known as the fuzzy degree of membership), so there may be overlaps.

In archaeometry, cluster analysis is a commonly applied method. Cluster analysis can be considered as a dimensionality reduction technique since it condenses the information into a graph where it is possible to appreciate the formation of the groups. Unfortunately, this traditional clustering method and derived techniques have several drawbacks. One of the problems is that many of these algorithms implicitly impose a model of fixed geometric nature (known as an objective function) to detect the clusters that will be formed, regardless of the underlying distribution of the data in n-dimensional space (Handl et al., 2005; Thrun, 2018). Because they are dependent on the transformation applied to the data, different clustering algorithms typically give very different results or detect clusters even if the distribution of the data is random, as most of these methods classify data based on the similarities between pairs of objects determined by a metric and using different criteria for merging or nesting clusters.

In addition, these analyses are unstable when the researcher chooses to add new cases or delete some. This happens because, when varying the cases, the calculation of distances changes, so the configurations of the clusters will also change. Another disadvantage is that these classic techniques do not offer any guidance for choosing the "optimal" number of groups, such as the level at which the dendrogram should be cut. On the other hand, with nonhierarchical clustering techniques, it is necessary to provide a priori the number of groups, which in most cases is unknown. Also, they are not robust in the presence of outliers. In the case of hierarchical clustering techniques, since they are rigid partitioning methods, once a data point is assigned to a cluster, it will not be considered again, which means that hierarchical algorithms are not able to correct potential classification errors. It is evident that classic clustering techniques have a series of disadvantages. In short, it can be stated that "these techniques do not provide a consistent way to predict the probability or membership of data belonging to existing groups" (Heller, 2007, p. 12).

Cluster analysis is considered a step in the knowledge discovery process (Thrun & Ultsch, 2021). Currently, clustering algorithms relate the classification problem to the discovery of *natural clusters* in data. The characteristic of natural clusters is that the subsets are clearly defined in the data and do not need to be dissected. Thrun (2018) defines natural clusters as those that are characterized by a discontinuity that can be based on distance or density. Those that are based on distance are defined as compact structures with small intra-cluster distances and large inter-cluster distances. In these, there are continuous regions of high-dimensional space represented by medium or densely populated point clouds that are surrounded by continuous and relatively empty regions of space. On the other hand, natural clusters defined by their density are based on the idea of neighborhoods present between experimental units, which can result in one-way or multi-directional neighborhoods.

Current algorithms have several advantages that allow the recognition of such clusters, greatly facilitating the understanding of the relationships between all the elements of the research and allowing a good generalization or prediction about the attributes. As a projection method, it is advisable to use a nonlinear and parameter-free method. For this, in this Element we recommend using projection-based clustering known as databionic swarm, or DBS (Thrun, 2018; Thrun & Ultsch, 2021), which is a clustering method that projects the high-dimensional points into two dimensions using the conversion of distances or dissimilarities. In other words, the swarm projects high-dimensional data onto a two-dimensional plane by using intelligent agents working in a toroidal and polar network. This results in a three-dimensional topographic map from a self-organized, simplified emergent map with hypsometric colors and with reliefs derived from the unified distance matrix of projected points.

The topographic map can be described as a 3D virtual landscape with a specific color scale that defines the contour lines, where the valleys or basins represent the groups, and the hills and mountains surrounding the basins represent the boundaries between the groups (López-García et al., 2020; Thrun, 2018). The optimal number of clusters can be visually estimated with the help of the map. Moreover, DBS can detect the absence of natural groups in the data (i.e., when the data is not groupable). The DBS method can be implemented using the R package **DatabionicSwarm** (Thrun, 2025). For more details on the theory and implementation of the algorithm, see Thrun (2018) and López-García et al. (2024); for its application in archaeology, see López-García et al. (2020) and Argote et al. (2024). It can also be consulted on the website of the algorithm developer, Michael Thrun, at https://cran.r-project.org/web/packages/DatabionicSwarm/index.html.

In general, in the process of discovering if the data present a group structure, there are three different classification methods: unsupervised classification, supervised classification, and semi-supervised classification, which is halfway between the previous two. In unsupervised classification, also known as clustering, no a priori class of the data is established during the classification processes. The partitions are established using a distance criterion to quantify the similarity between the observations so that observations within the same group are similar to each other and different from observations found in the other groups. In contrast, supervised classification methods are based on a set of previously known classes to cluster the samples that are labeled as belonging to two or more classes, intending to predict the correct class of the data without labeling the correct structure of the groups. Linear discriminant analysis is a clear example of this type of classification. However, this method assumes homogeneity of the covariance matrices of the groups, and continuous variables must follow a multivariate normal distribution – two conditions that are difficult to fulfil.

Halfway between both methods is semi-supervised classification, which is a learning model for both labeled and unlabeled data. In this, labeled data are used to train a classifier to determine the allocation of unlabeled samples into pre-established groups. Since the objective of provenance is to associate data of unknown origin with predefined groups or classes, for example, data from raw material deposits (labeled data) and artifacts of unidentified source (unlabeled data), then we are dealing with a problem of partial labeling of the data, therefore leading us to semi-supervised classification. In the following section, this method is explained in detail.

7.1 Semi-Supervised Classification

For determining the provenance of artifacts, archaeologists collect samples directly from the assumed sources of raw material as a reference to associate them with the objects of unknown origin, commonly applying bivariate or multivariate analyses as tools. But, as mentioned above, these procedures cause overlaps between different groups, and it is more complicated to assign the samples to the deposits if the analytical technique is less conclusive. If samples of known origin are available, semi-supervised classification techniques are ideal for generating a model to assign samples of unknown origin to groups of samples with known origin.

Semi-supervised learning is very useful in machine learning and pattern recognition because it uses unlabeled data (i.e., artifacts recovered from archaeological sites) to improve supervised learning tasks when a small number of labeled data (raw material source samples) are available; hence, this method is known as partially supervised mixture modeling (Bouveyron et al., 2019; Krijthe, 2016; McLachlan & Peel, 2000). In this paradigm, it is assumed that the number of data to be labeled is greater than the number of data already labeled (Zhu & Goldberg, 2009). Instead of fitting a model using only labeled data or training data, as in DA, in semi-supervised methods both training data and unlabeled data (or test data) are used in model fitting to predict class labels from unlabeled data. It is from these two subsets of data that a classifier $\hat{f}$ is trained, which allows better performance than that of a supervised classifier trained only with labeled data.

Many of these algorithms assume finite mixed Gaussian distributions for clustering; in the case of partial labeling, a semi-supervised analogue of MBC is used (Dang et al., 2019). In the adjustment of the mixture models, the observations are assigned a label that is the most likely a posteriori depending on the selected model and its estimated parameters (Baudry et al., 2010). Several approaches have been proposed that follow the semi-supervised classification paradigm, most of which follow the generative paradigm. For details on fitting this variant of the finite mixture model, see Banfield and Raftery (1993) and Celeux and Govaert (1995). For reasons of simplicity, here we only detail some of the easiest packages for archaeologists to use.

Rmixmod (Lebret et al., 2015) is an exploratory data analysis tool for solving cluster analysis and supervised problems by fitting a mixture model with Gaussian mixture distributions. It can be used in semi-supervised situations where the dataset is partially labeled. **Rmixmod** takes as arguments one matrix of data with labels and another matrix with data whose labels are unknown, assuming that each x_i arises from a population described by a probability density function. This probability density function is a finite mixture of density functions of parametric components, where each component models one of the K groups; this model fits the data for maximum likelihood. The membership of the observations in one of the K groups can be estimated by means of a rule called maximum a posteriori probability, which considers the conditional probability that observation x_i arises from group k (Lebret et al., 2015). Semi-supervised classification in **Rmixmod** is accomplished by calling two functions: mixmodLearn() and mixmodPredict().

The first function requires two essential arguments to be able to run: an array of *X* data and a vector containing the known labels *z*. This function can be combined with other instances to maximize classification performance. Creating an instance of the '[GaussianModel]' class with the 'mixmodGaussianModel' function allows you to define a list of 28 Gaussian models to test in the classification, from which the most suitable model will be selected based on selection criteria that measure the goodness of fit of a statistical model (i.e., BIC or cross-validation [CV]). The arguments in this function define a family of models (general, diagonal, and spherical):

$$\text{mixmodGaussianModel (family} = \text{"all", listModels} = \text{NULL, free.} \\ \text{proportions} = \text{TRUE, equal.proportions} = \text{TRUE)}. \tag{7}$$

Forcing this argument to "all" instructs the program to test all models: those that impose spherical covariance matrices, those that impose diagonal covariance matrices, and those models with variable proportions, volume, and orientation. **Rmixmod** uses the EM algorithm to obtain parameter estimates for mixed models (Dempster et al., 1977). The EM algorithm is applied in situations where one wishes to estimate a set of θ parameters that describe an underlying probability distribution, given only an observed part of the complete data produced by the distribution. It consists of two steps: step E and step M. Step E (expectation) calculates the probability that each of the observations belongs to one of the Gaussians; step M (maximization) maximizes the likelihood function with the probabilities calculated in step E, obtaining a new set of parameters that are used to update the conditional expectation estimate of the unknown data in the next iteration. The values obtained in step M provide the posterior probability that observation x_i belongs to group *k* (Cribbin, 2008). Steps E and M are repeated iteratively until the likelihood converges (Lerdo de Tejada Pavón, 2014).

At the end of the process, the 'mixmodLearn()' function returns an instance of the 'mixmodLearn' class. Its two attributes will have the following outputs:

- *Results*: a list of MixmodResults objects containing all the results sorted in ascending order according to the given criterion (in descending order in the CV criterion);
- *bestResult*: a MixmodResults object that includes the best results from the model fitting.

Regarding the second function, mixmodPredict(), it only needs two arguments: an array of data from the unlabeled observations and a classification rule that extracts the parameters obtained with the 'bestResult' attribute to make the prediction. The algorithm returns an instance of the MixmodPredict class containing predicted partitions and probabilities (Langrognet et al., 2025). For the classification of partial data, there are two criteria: BIC and CV. For BIC, the log-likelihood of partial labeling must be used, where all the tags known as a priori (z^l) remain fixed in step E of the EM algorithm (Lebret et al., 2015). As for CV, which is the default criterion, this is a technique for evaluating how the results of a statistical analysis generalize to a set of independent data. What it does is form a subgroup and call it a training set and validate it with another subgroup called a test set. By using random partitions in V-blocks of approximately equal sizes, it obtains unbiased estimates of the error rate (Lebret et al., 2015). The classification rule used in the model adjustment includes the number of clusters, the selected model, and the best parameters of the model using the criteria (BIC or CV); under this scheme, it is possible to select the criterion that gives the best configuration.

Finally, for displaying the estimated classification structure, we recommend using the R package **ClusVis**, which performs a Gaussian-based visualization using the conditional memberships of the model fitted to the input data. The algorithm rests on the assumption that only one display output projected on a plane R^2 must match the mixture of the input classification; this is justified because both objects involved are of the same nature (i.e., they are probabilistic objects) (Biernacki et al., 2021). The output of the mixture includes spherical Gaussian components with the same number of components as the initial clustering mixture. The accuracy of the mapping from the original mixture space (f) to the final mixture space ($\hat{g}$) is evaluated through the normalized entropy difference $\delta_E(f, \hat{g})$. The range of normalized entropy values is $[-1, 0, 1]$, with $\delta_E = 0$ being the most accurate value in terms of mapping accuracy between the overlap of components f and ($\hat{g}$). Like other projection methods, the percentage of inertia per axis can also be used as a measure of mapping quality, with the closest to 100% being the best fit of the model.

The **ClusVis** function requires two parameters: the logarithm of the classification probabilities of each specimen and the proportion of the mixture. By specifying the option add.obs = FALSE, the graph will represent the overlap between the groups. Each group is represented by its centers, with a 95% confidence level border. For further details on the implementation of the R package **Rmixmod**, see (Langrognet et al., 2025); for the Gaussian-based visualization (**ClusVis**), see (Biernacki et al., 2021).

8 Model Validation

In most archaeometry research, exploratory techniques are used without validating the results. However, the validation of statistical results is a mandatory process that allows the confirmation of the initial research hypotheses and statistically verifies the clustering or classification obtained, since many traditional clustering algorithms can generate a partition of the sample space regardless of whether the data have a clusterable structure (Duda et al., 2001; Xu & Wunsch, 2005). These methods impose certain constraints on the behavior of the data and, if the actual clusters in the data do not match the target function of the clustering algorithm and have another geometric shape, then the data is forced to match the target function of the algorithm, producing misleading results (Thrun, 2018). For example, Ward's method only works efficiently when clusters are spherical and leads to misclassifications when clusters deviate from this assumption, as well as not being robust in the presence of outliers.

Similarly, the K-means method also assumes spherical clusters, depends on the initialization of the algorithm, must specify in advance the number of clusters, usually has problems clustering data if the groups are of different sizes and densities, and cannot operate with noisy data and outliers; also, its search is prone to getting stuck in local minimums. In addition to the above, traditional clustering algorithms do not explicitly establish the number of clusters (Heller, 2007). That is, although the dendrogram helps to represent the hierarchical process of clustering, the number of groups varies depending on where the tree is pruned; if the number of observations is very large, it is more difficult to appreciate the relationship between the experimental units and the number of clusters. In addition, these algorithms are not robust, so if new units of analysis are added, the results are disturbed by producing different results.

In contrast, when using linear projection methods, the quality of the projection and, consequently, the visualization will depend on the transformation of the data and the concept of similarity chosen as the basis of the objective function (Thrun, 2018). It is important to note that PCA is only a dimensionality reduction technique that allows data to be represented in two or three dimensions, considering that two or three factorial axes are preserved in which variance is maximized. However, this technique does not define groups explicitly and, therefore, its results should not be relied on much. Thus, traditional algorithms do not "define a probabilistic model of the data, so it is hard to ask how 'good' a clustering is, compare it to other models, make predictions and cluster new data into an existing hierarchy" (Heller, 2007, p. 27). Consequently, the resulting clustering scheme requires some sort of evaluation to assess its validity.

Given these weaknesses, an integral step in clustering/classification is the statistical validation of results; here, validation criteria provide insight into the quality of the clustering solutions. To validate the clustering, questions must be answered, such as: Are the groups obtained significant? Are we looking at artifacts produced by the algorithm? What is the optimal number of groups in the data? With validation, it is possible to check whether the procedure is correct and whether the data fit the model. The inferences produced can have a high degree of certainty, putting the entire interpretation at risk if incorrect information is used. In the published literature, a wide variety of validation indices has been proposed for nonparametric methods, including external, relative, and internal criteria, which are thoroughly explained in Gordon (1998) and Jain and Dubes (1988). Up to 42 internal indexes and 11 external indexes for cluster validation can be found in **clValid**, an R package for cluster validation (Brock et al., 2008), and the package **clusterCrit** (Desgraupes, 2018).

A useful tool is the silhouette chart, which is an unsupervised clustering index for assessing the quality of a cluster and identifying the optimal number of clusters (Kaufman & Rousseeuw, 2005; Rousseeuw, 1987). The silhouette value varies from −1 to +1, where positive values close to +1 specify that the samples are well assigned to their own cluster; if the value is 0, it means that the sample is between two groups, and samples with negative values (<0) are probably in the wrong group. Another graphical representation for visualizing high-dimensional data is the heat map (Wilkinson & Friendly, 2009), which visualizes the distances ordered by the clustering through variations in color, placing variables in the rows and columns and coloring the cells within the table. Heat maps are good for showing how similar the objects are within a cluster and how dissimilar they are outside a cluster. To obtain heat maps and silhouette plots, the package **DataVisualizations** version 1.3.3 (Thrun & Ultsch, 2018; Thrun et al., 2025) can be used.

If you want to get a rough idea of the optimal number of clusters in a partition of a dataset, you can use several indexes that are freely available for the R environment. The **NbClust** package (Charrad et al., 2014) provides 30 indices that determine the number of clusters in a dataset. In the case of fuzzy clustering, the packages **advclust** (Bagus & Pramana, 2016) or **fcvalid** (Cebeci, 2020) can be used, providing 18 internal indexes to validate the results of fuzzy clustering algorithms. Also, a supervised index can be used to assess the efficiency of the classifications, with accuracy being the simplest example (Thrun, 2018), which is defined as follows:

$$1 - \text{Accuracy}[\%] = \frac{[\text{No. of true positives}]}{[\text{No. of cases}]}. \tag{8}$$

In Equation 8, the number of true positives refers to the number of labeled data points for which the label defined by a priori classification is identical to the label defined after the clustering process, and the denominator only refers to the total number of cases. This index is defined as one minus the accuracy, so if the classification is correct, the resulting value will be close to 100%, and if the value is 50% or less, the result is attributable to chance (Thrun, 2018).

9 Compositional Study of Archaeological Pottery: Example for Variable Selection

García-Heras et al. (2001) state that the fundamental goal of compositional analysis studies as a means of defining the provenance of archaeological materials is to isolate sample assemblages that show similar geochemical profiles. Furthermore, once the groups have been obtained, they must be statistically validated. This statement implies that the identified subsets must be mutually exclusive; the specimens in each group or subgroup must be sufficiently related to each other and totally different from the specimens from the rest of the groups. The identified compositional groups form what are known as reference groups, which can be used to classify artifacts of unknown origin to determine their provenance. This type of study applied to obsidian artifacts has generally had good results, since obsidian is a geological material with a significantly homogeneous composition.

Still, as discussed in Section 1, processing data by classical statistical methods has not been the most adequate. When reviewing published literature regarding the compositional analysis of pottery, the picture is much more complicated than in obsidian analyses, not least because of the greater heterogeneity of its components. Some of the unknowns to be solved when establishing reference groups are whether the ceramic types were locally produced or imported and whether the different manufacturing recipes can be distinguished. However, we found that many studies present overlaps between the reference groups, which causes greater confusion in the classification of these materials.

In the context of ceramic analyses, two scenarios can be found. In the first, there are datasets that form compact and well-differentiated groups, which allow the artifacts to be related to their sites without any problem or to define the recipe used for the manufacture of each ceramic group, which is different from that of the other groups. In the second scenario, there may be overlapping regions where the experimental units cannot be precisely defined because they have some degree of intersection with other groups, which causes the data points to have partial membership of more than one group. This means that the groups share common characteristics, for example, that the clay banks used for manufacturing the pieces are the same, or that the recipe used in the production of the ceramic paste is common in some ceramic types analyzed, differing only for stylistic reasons. If the intention is to detect differences in the composition of the ceramics according to the variability of each group, it is necessary to have a strategy capable of finding significant structures in the data.

To exemplify the procedures proposed in this Element and the efficiency of variable selection methods, we will reanalyze a published dataset where it is difficult to appreciate the formation of groups due to the excessive overlaps that occur between the data. For this section, we use a database published by Harry, Fish, and Fish (2002) that corresponds to a study on the production and distribution of pottery from two Hohokam settlements of the early Classic period (ca. 1100–1300 AD), the Marana and Los Robles communities, located in southern Arizona. The purpose of their study was to understand how the production of Tanque Verde red-on-brown pottery was organized and differentially distributed between these two communities. The samples were the result of combining the materials of this ceramic type collected and analyzed with NAA by two different research projects. The first set corresponded to $n = 360$ samples (Fish et al., 1992), later increased by adding another $n = 361$ samples (Harry, 1997). Of this total of $n = 721$ samples, $n = 558$ came from the communities of Marana and Los Robles. As a complement to chemical studies, Harry, Fish and Fish (2002) analyzed $n = 413$ samples mineralogically. The data can be downloaded from the database of the University of Missouri Research Reactor (MURR) Archaeometry Laboratory, under the direction of Dr. Michael Glascock, at https://archaeometry.missouri.edu/murr_database.html.

The authors applied PCA and projected the first two PCs, sustaining the ability to discriminate $K = 8$ compositional groups, which they labeled A, BC, E, F, G, South Tucson, Phoenix, and Papagueria, in addition to a large number of unassigned samples (Table 2). From their results, they concluded that the communities of Marana and Los Robles were best represented in five of these groups (A, BC, E, F, and G), and that groups Phoenix, Papagueria, and F had the most distinct chemical groups, while the rest of the groups presented overlaps. It

Table 2 Number of samples assigned to each of the reference groups (Harry, Fish & Fish, 2002)

Compositional group	n
A	107
BC	125
E	31
F	20
G	39
South Tucson	23
Phoenix	11
Papagueria	26
Unassigned	339
Total	**721**

should be noted that, although the authors claim to have charted the eight compositional groups, in the original graph they only included five (A, BC, E, F, and G), and it is not possible to know if this was just a publication error. Subsequently, the authors used discriminant analysis including only groups A, BC, E, F, and G, achieving better separation between the groups. Even so, the only group without overlap was BC; there was a slight overlap between groups A and E, and a pronounced overlap between groups F and G. The authors concluded that the overlaps were due to the chemical similarity in the alluvial clays of these groups, such that groups A through G, in addition to South Tucson, were produced in the same general region.

While assessing the publication, we detected various problems, among which we can list the following:

1. The authors had a large number of values below the LOD, which they substituted using the Mahalanobis distance.
2. The data were transformed into $\log_{10}$.
3. There was no diagnosis of the existence of outliers.
4. All the components ($D = 32$ elements) were included in the analysis; they used PCA as a dimensionality reduction method.
5. To classify the samples, they applied the LDA method.
6. To validate their results, they used the Mahalanobis distance to calculate probabilities of belonging to the groups, using $D = 32$ components for the groups with a sufficiently large sample size (A, BC, and G) and the first 13 principal components for the groups with small sample sizes (E and F). For the Phoenix group, whose sample size was small, the Mahalanobis distance was not used; however, the authors argued that their separation was achieved by using other projections.

To replicate the procedure of Harry, Fish, and Fish (2002), we first replaced the missing values using the Mahalanobis distance, and then applied PCA to these data using the software of the MURR Archaeometry Laboratory, Gauss Runtime, and C statistical routines v8.8c (Glascock, 2021; Glascock, 2022). The only difference was that we included the eight ceramic types reported by the authors. The result can be seen in Figure 1. The variance explained by the first two PCs was only 42.2% of the total variability, which reflects poor adjustment. This can also be seen in the projection in a graph of the points of the first two PCs (see the left image in Figure 1); here, the absence of a defined pattern in the data is clear. In the plot of PC1 vs. PC3 (see the right image in Figure 1), it can be observed that some samples are separated from the main group. However, a large number of peripheral observations can also be seen that are most likely outliers.

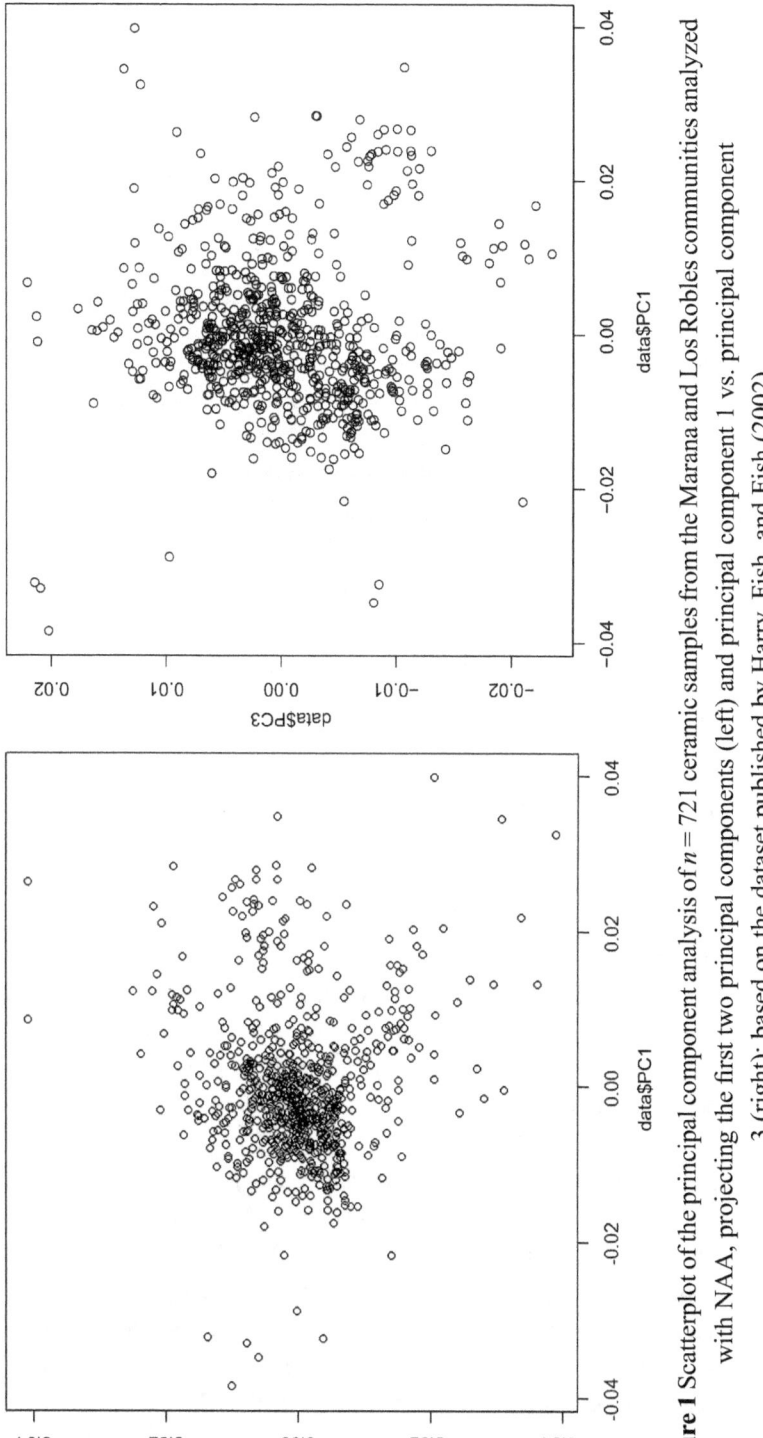

Figure 1 Scatterplot of the principal component analysis of $n = 721$ ceramic samples from the Marana and Los Robles communities analyzed with NAA, projecting the first two principal components (left) and principal component 1 vs. principal component 3 (right); based on the dataset published by Harry, Fish, and Fish (2002).

In their analysis, the authors found that 47% of the samples could not be assigned to any of the reference groups and assured that this could be a consequence of the fact that these samples corresponded to other ceramic types not considered in the analysis, to outliers in the recorded groups, or to pastes prepared differently and whose compositional similarity with the existing groups was altered. To assign samples to groups, the authors used the probability estimation of the Mahalanobis distance by setting the *p*-value thresholds at 0.0001% and 0.0002%; they stated that, as the Mahalanobis distance had an abrupt decrease, the unassigned samples showed a low probability of belonging to any of the established groups. It should be clarified that, when using the Mahalanobis distance to classify each of the sample units as belonging to one of K classes, the covariance matrix of each class must be estimated; then, the Mahalanobis distance is calculated for each class, and the experimental sample is assigned to the class for which the distance is minimal.

To calculate relative probabilities from the Mahalanobis distance, the assumption that the variables have a normal distribution must be respected, since the sum of squares that determines the chi-square value is calculated directly from the Mahalanobis distance for each data point. Glascock et al. (1998) are very clear in stating that "if the assumption of normality is violated, the probabilities of belonging to some groups may be exaggerated while the probabilities of other groups may be underestimated" (p. 31). In addition, Etherington (2019), when describing the use of a chi-square distribution to convert Mahalanobis distances into probabilities, experimentally demonstrated that there is an error that is constantly made in the calculation of probabilities. This consists of assuming that Mahalanobis distances are distributed like chi-square, with n − 1 degrees of freedom, which is erroneous. In reality, Mahalanobis distance values follow a chi-square distribution with degrees of freedom equal to n. If this correction is not made in the calculation of the probabilities, a bad adjustment will be obtained that underestimates the probability of belonging to one of the K classes, causing a mistaken prediction of the samples.

Finally, outliers are known to have a strong impact on location and dispersion matrix estimates, with a single outlier having the ability to bias calculations related to the sample covariance matrix (Hubert & Van der Veeken, 2008). In addition, compositional data rarely have a normal distribution. All the above together can cause a misassignment of the units to the groups when using the Mahalanobis distance. First, it is important to check if your data has a cluster structure. This can be easily verified by generating the silhouette coefficient used by Harry, Fish, and Fish (2002), following their procedure and transforming the $D = 32$ components to $\log_{10}$. In this way, the graph corresponding to

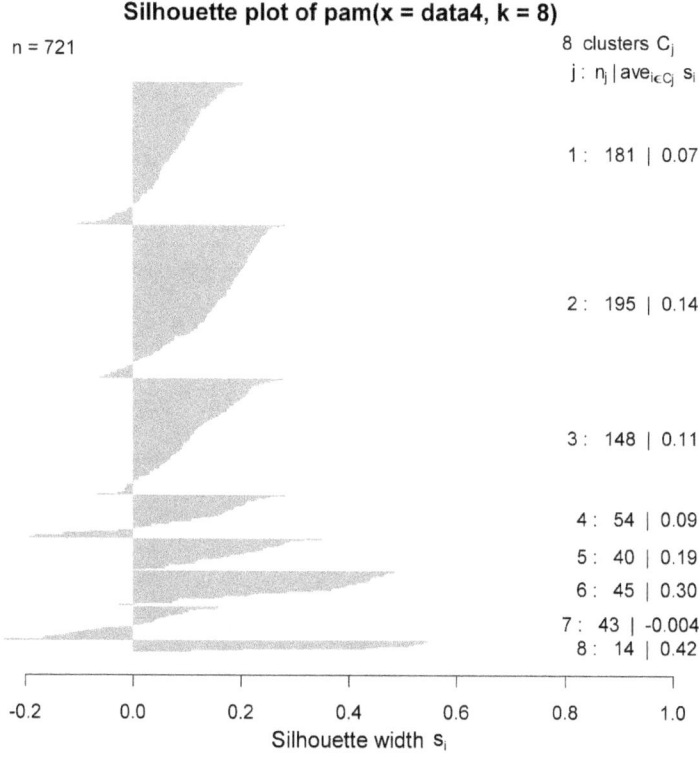

Figure 2 Silhouette plot of the Hohokam communities dataset (Harry, Fish & Fish, 2002), showing various problematic points for $K = 8$.

Figure 2 will be obtained, denoting whether the groups are poorly represented and whether there is a large amount of data assigned to the incorrect clusters (represented by the number of negative values of S_i in each group). Another piece of evidence of a lack of fit is the average silhouette value. In the case of Harry, Fish, and Fish, the average silhouette value is only 0.12, while adequate grouping is characterized by an average silhouette value greater than 0.5. Any value below 0.2 should be interpreted as the absence of a substantial cluster structure (Everitt et al., 2011; Thrun, 2018). In this way, this simple test shows whether there are problems with the assignment of units to groups.

When data are generated from multiple clusters, the pairwise distances and distributions of the first PC (which accounts for the maximum variation in the data) must be multimodal (Adolfsson et al., 2019). Figure 3 shows the frequency distribution of the first PC of this dataset, which shows unimodal distribution, suggesting that the data cannot be clustered. If the data do not

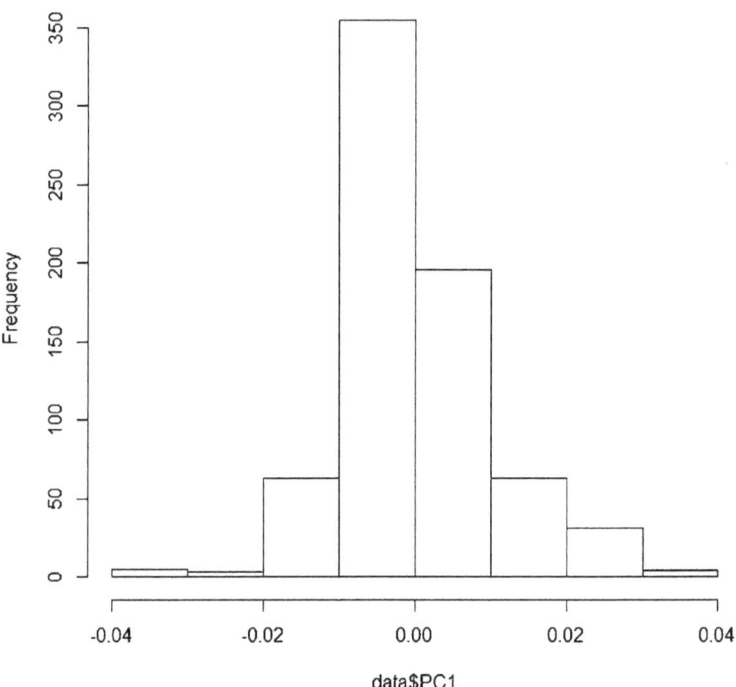

Figure 3 Frequency distribution plot of the first principal component of the neutronic activation analysis of ceramic sherds from the Marana and Los Robles communities, based on the dataset published by Harry, Fish, and Fish (2002).

have an underlying cluster structure to be partitioned in a meaningful way, the clustering may be incorrect for the data under experimentation or "the data may need to be reprocessed. Otherwise, if the data is found to be clusterable, a clustering algorithm may be selected or developed" (Adolfsson et al., 2019, p. 2). Some of the causes of the poor fit achieved in this case may be the type of preprocessing used, the presence of outliers, the low adaptability of the PCA to nonlinear data structures, and the inclusion of irrelevant and noisy variables that can mask the underlying structure of the data.

The methodology proposed in this Element aims to search for natural groups in the data based on the eight assumptions of the statistical treatment of compositional data (established in Sections 2 to 8 of this Element) in order to correctly solve the classification problem, considering everything from the transformation of the data to the validation. Following its respective steps, the values with a low LOD were first imputed; for this, the simulation-based data augmentation algorithm of the **zCompositions** package was used to impute the left-censored values. Table 3 specifies the components with values < LOD and the number of imputed values in each component; since there were Ni values < LOD in most of the samples, this component was completely removed from the analysis. Secondly, the diagnosis of the data was made using the Donoho–Stahel outlyingness measure with the R package **robustbase**, which considers skewness. This procedure identified $n = 11$ data points whose behavior was far from the regular observations. The outliers corresponded to observations 4, 6, 211, 235, 238, 245, 270, 294, 323, 626, and 668, which were removed from the matrix.

The third step was to transform the data matrix without outliers using the centered log ratio (clr); the transformed matrix was used to apply three variable selection models, setting the K number of groups between 2 and 9. The results of all three methods are summarized in Table 4, showing the variables selected by

Table 3 Components with values < LOD and number of imputed values from the data published in Harry, Fish, and Fish (2002)

Component	Number of values below the LOD
Co	6
Eu	8
Sb	14
Zn	26
Ni	486
Total	**540**

Table 4 Variable selection methods presenting the selected variables, the number of clusters, and their accuracy

Feature selection method	Number of clusters	Selected variables	Accuracy
SelvarMix	8	As, La, Lu, Nd, Sm, U, Co, Cr, Cs, Fe, Hf, Rb, Sb, Sc, Sr, Th, Al	99.01%
VarSelLCM	4	Cs, Cr, Co, Sb, Sr, Na, Lu, Yb, V, Fe, As, Ca, Sc, Dy, U, Th, Rb, Ti, Mn, Ta	91.96%
clustvarsel	9	Cr, Sb, Rb, Cs, Fe, Sc, Co, Na, Eu, Ta	85.61%

each method and the number of clusters suggested. The right-hand column presents the accuracy obtained after projecting the data using only the variables selected by each method. The first method was **SelvarMix**, which was applied in combination with the **Rmixmod** package, considering $m = 28$ Gaussian mixture forms using the 'mixmodGaussianModel' function; the selection criteria of the BIC model was used. In this case, of the 28 candidate models, the one that best fit was the model = Gaussian_pk_lk_D_Ak_D (volume = free, shape = free, orientation = equal). The output of the program provides the roles of each variable – the variables relevant to the grouping (S), the redundant variables (U), and the independent variables (W) – as well as the number of groups and the assignment of each of the units to the K groups. For the data published by Harry, Fish, and Fish (2002), it was found that the best partition was for $K = 8$ and that the relevant variables corresponded to only 17 of the 31 input variables, with the rest being irrelevant variables.

Establishing the parameters in the same way as with the previous method, the **VarSelLCM** method retained 20 relevant variables (see Table 4), proposing only $K = 4$ clusters. However, the accuracy result is lower than with **SelvarMix** and its silhouette plot and heat map (Figure 4) show a bad fit (with silhouette values below 0.5), suggesting that both the partition and the number of clusters are not adequate. The **clustvarsel** method depends on the **mclust** package, in which the volume, shape, and orientation of the covariances can be constrained to be equal or variable across groups. An advantage of the **mclust** package is that it allows the automatic selection of the number of components and the selection of parsimonious covariance structures (Scrucca & Raftery, 2018), so that a family of $m = 14$ possible models with different geometric characteristics can be specified. For this method, the parameters set were: $K = 2: 9$, search = c ("greedy", "headlong"), and direction = c("forward", "backward").

Clustvarsel only retained 10 components as relevant variables of the total $D = 31$, whether they were independent of the clustering variables or correlated. The step-by-step algorithm was implemented forward and backward, and the best MBC (using the subset of selected relevant clustering variables) was the VEE parameterization from the **mclust** package, which corresponds to an ellipsoidal distribution of variable volume, equal shape, and equal orientation, with $K = 9$ clusters. Although its silhouette plot and heat map (Figure 5) showed a better performance than that of **VarSelLCM**, with a silhouette value above 0.5, there were misassigned observations (indicated by silhouette values < 0); also, the accuracy obtained was the lowest of all three methods. As can be seen in Table 4, the method with the highest accuracy was the **SelvarMix** method, which reached 99.01% accuracy; the method that followed was **clustvarsel**, with 91.96% accuracy, and, finally, the **VarSelLCM** method, with only 85.61%

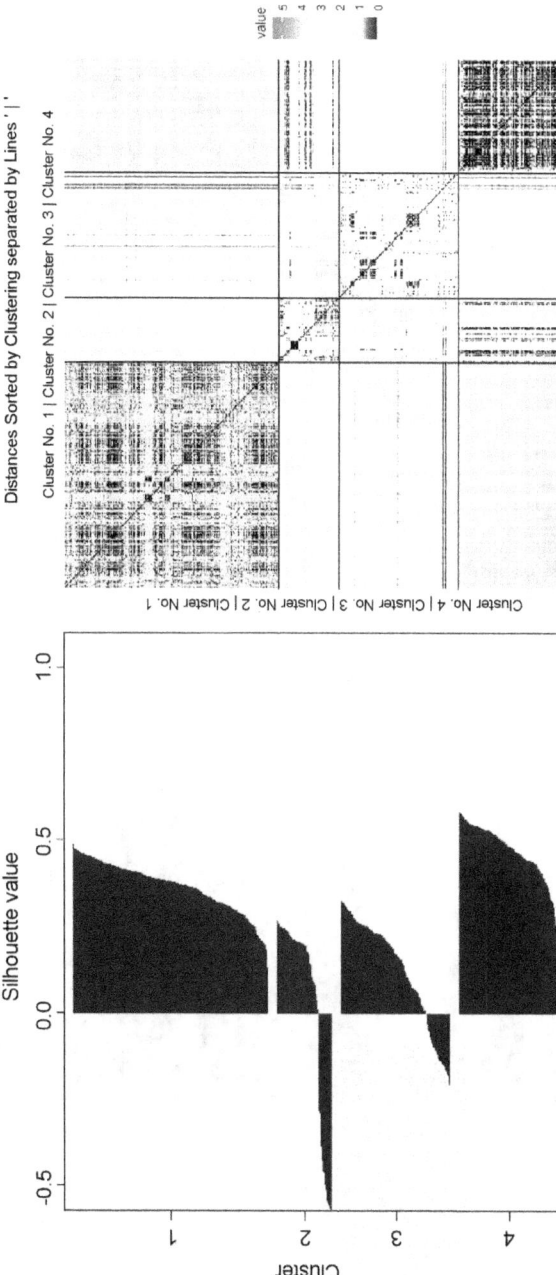

Figure 4 Silhouette plot (left) and heat map (right) of the clustering obtained with the VarSelLCM method. Color version available at www.cambridge.org/determining-provenance

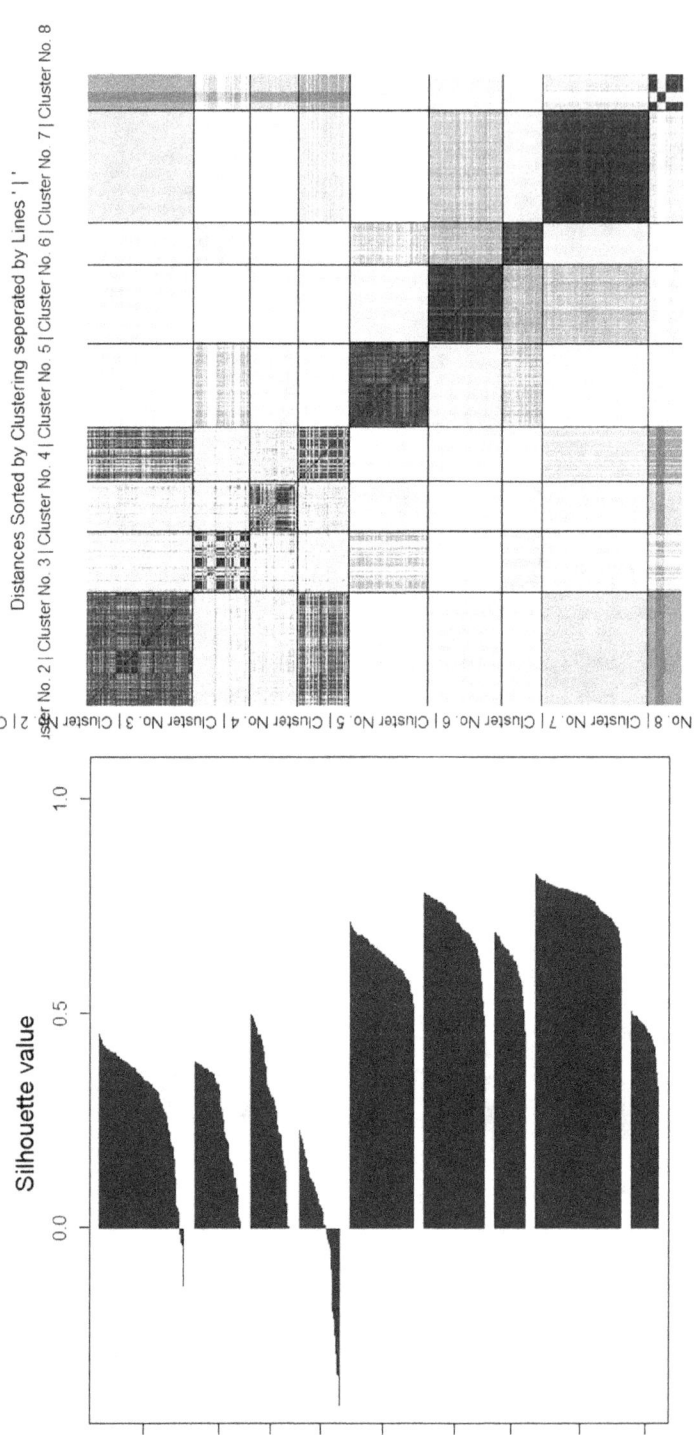

Figure 5 Silhouette plot (left) and heatmap (right) of the clustering obtained with the clustvarsel method. Color version available at www.cambridge.org/determining-provenance

accuracy. Based on this and the visualization of their corresponding silhouette plots and heat maps, it was decided to retain the **SelvarMix** model.

As a first step in the clustering, the components selected by the chosen variable selection method were used and the data were labeled according to the partition made by the algorithms. To project the set of variables and data obtained by the **SelvarMix** method, DBS was applied and the topographic map was visualized to see the structure and number of groups detected by the variable selection algorithm (Figure 6). In this map, if the cluster is valid, then each cluster should consist of a single connected area, the boundaries of which will be represented by mountain ranges (Thrun, 2018). The dots on the topographic map symbolize the ceramic samples, the similarities between the high-dimensional data are represented as valleys, and the differences between groups are represented as mountain ranges or ridges.

As can be seen in Figure 6, the high-dimensional structures of the reference groups are visible on the topographic map, where eight valleys can be identified, leading to the election of eight groups. The structures are clearly defined by discontinuity and can therefore be characterized as natural clusters. For this example, the clustering is valid because mountain ranges do not divide the groups and the distances within groups are smaller than the distances between groups.

As the topographic map is toroidal (i.e., where the edges of the grid are cyclically connected), it is possible to generate the 3D island-shaped landscape from the visualization of the previous topographic map. To do this, you first

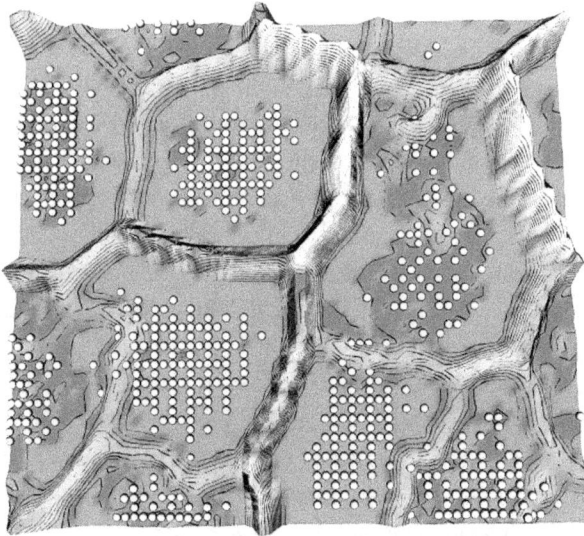

Figure 6 Toroidal map of the Tanque Verde red-on-brown pottery dataset displaying clear cluster structures with eight visible valleys.

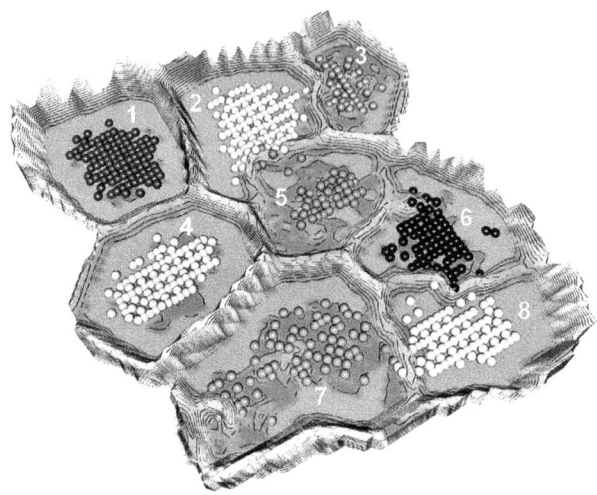

Figure 7 Topographic map of Tanque Verde red-on-brown pottery displaying clear cluster structures with eight visible valleys. The densest cluster with smaller intra-group distances is in dark blue (number 1). Color version available at www.cambridge.org/determining-provenance

must declare in the algorithm that $K = 8$ and then interactively cut the island around the mountain ranges; the result can be seen in Figure 7. This new topographic map allows us to visualize the 709 dimensional specimens colored according to their membership of one of the eight valleys: four larger clusters represented by light blue, green, dark blue, and black dots (numbers 2, 4, 1, and 6, respectively, in the grayscale image); three smaller clusters represented by gray, yellow, and red dots (number 3, 8, and 5, respectively, in the grayscale image), the latter two with some dots on the border; and one cluster represented by magenta dots (number 7 in the grayscale image), which is a little more scattered than in the other clusters. In addition to the topographic map, the groups can be deduced with the help of the dendrogram of the distances defined by the swarm (Figure 8), where the formation of eight groups can also be seen.

Finally, the respective heat map (Figure 9, right) and silhouette plot (Figure 9, left) were used to externally verify the clustering result. The heat map shows that this dataset is defined by discontinuities, as there are small distances within each group and large distances between the eight groups, confirming a clear group structure. On the other hand, the silhouette diagram visualizes the homogeneity of the DBS cluster structures. Therefore, the processed ceramic data is a dataset with natural groups that are specified by the chemical composition of the reference groups defined by discontinuities. However, some observations can be seen that are wrongly classified in groups 1 and 2, whose

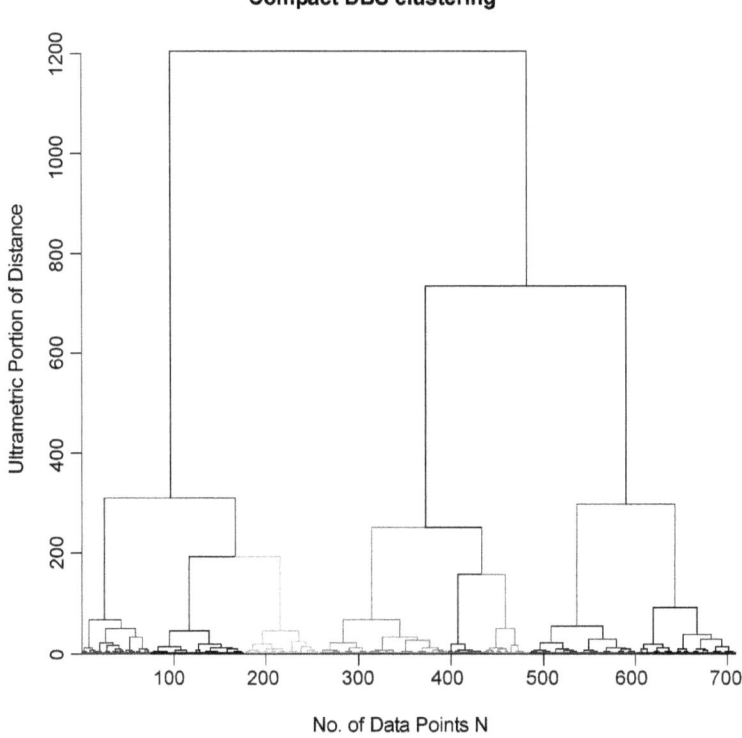

Figure 8 Dendrogram generated using DBS; the compact DBS clustering indicates eight clusters. Color version available at www.cambridge.org/determining-provenance

silhouette is negative. Even so, the clustering structure is considered homogeneous since most of the data points (y-axis) are above 0.5 (x-axis), showing that the clustering results for all eight clusters are valid.

The clusters detected have a significant interpretation in terms of their chemical composition, with the SRUW being an effective model to define the roles of the variables in the contexts of classification and clustering based on the Gaussian model. The good performance of the SelvarClust function was due to the fact that it adjusts a greater number of models, allowing the selection of the most parsimonious model and providing improved clustering partitions. This shows that, when all the variables are simultaneously included in a multivariate analysis, many are uninformative, causing greater complexity of the model since many variables do not provide information to the clustering. Although the **clustvarsel** method achieved a high percentage of accuracy, when projecting the data and validating the results, the groups did not appear clearly separated and a number of misassigned observations were observed (see Figure 5).

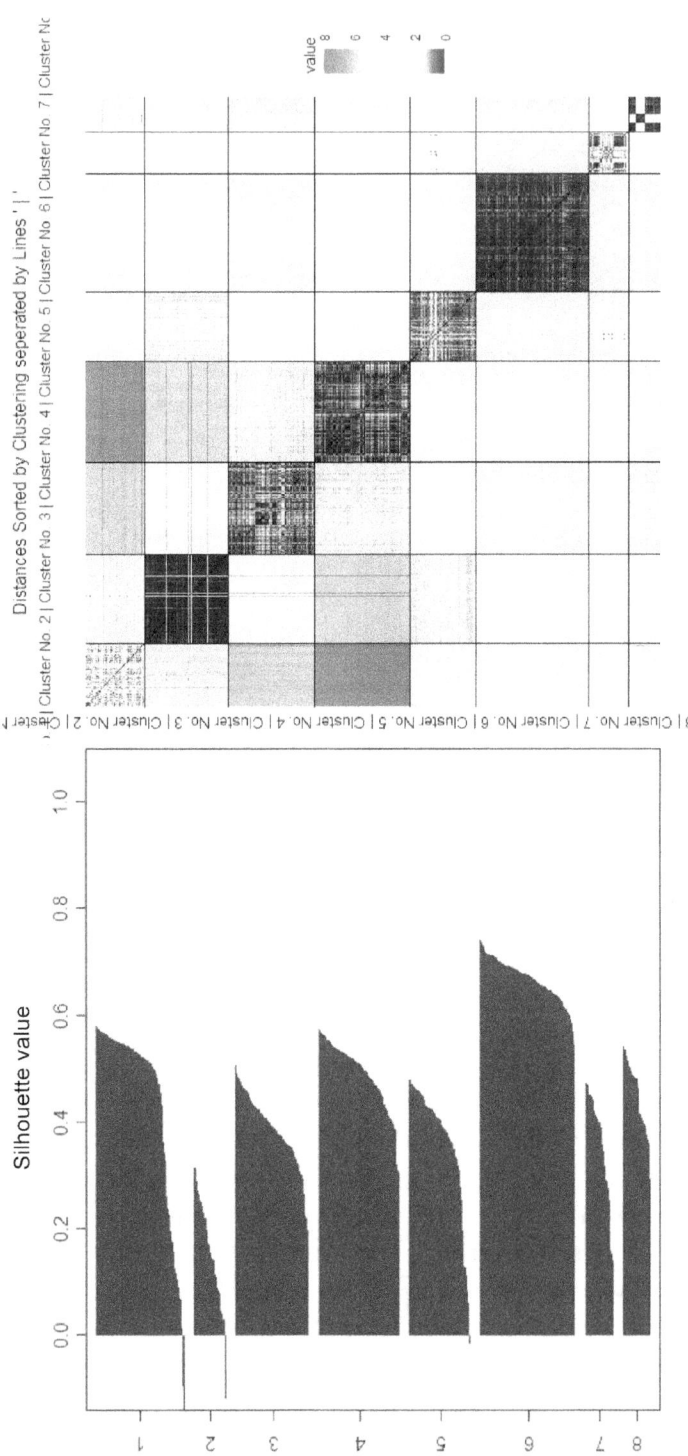

Figure 9 Silhouette plot of DBS clustering (left) and heat map of the distances about the eight identified clusters of the Tanque Verde red-on-brown pottery (right). Color version available at www.cambridge.org/determining-provenance

One cause of its poor fitness is that the **clustvarsel** algorithm uses step regression for the inclusion or exclusion of variables, and this procedure can suffer instability, although this is not very common (Scrucca & Raftery, 2018). On the other hand, the **VarSelLCM** and **clustvarsel** algorithms from the **mclust** package are greedy, needing multiple calls of the EM algorithm, and the automatic selection of the number of components in the mixture and the selection of covariance structures consists of only $m = 14$ parameterizations, unlike **SelvarMix**, which provides $m = 28$ models available in the **Rmixmod** package. Another reason for the poor fit of the **VarSelLCM** package for this exercise is because a Gaussian mixture model with the assumption of conditional independence is used for its selection of variables – a situation that is not fulfilled since there is a correlation between the adjacent ceramic groups.

It should be noted that the procedure used in this exercise is focused on the search for natural groups and, therefore, it is not up to us to make any type of interpretation of the data. From the results, we can only appreciate that the classification made by Harry, Fish, and Fish (2002) is different from the one obtained with the procedure proposed here. First, having set from the outset that the possible number of groups was in the range of two as a minimum and nine as a maximum, the partition made by the variable selection algorithm (and validated by the indices) concluded that $K = 8$ for this dataset. Although this number of groups is the same as in Harry, Fish, and Fish (2002), these authors had a large number of unassigned samples ($n = 339$), a situation that did not occur in our exercise. Another difference was that the Phoenix and Papagueria ceramic types, which the authors considered chemically distinct, were concentrated in a single group in our analysis.

Table 5 shows the total number of samples for each of the groups using variable selection and projection-based clustering. Of these, in group A, Harry, Fish, and Fish (2002) originally included a total of 107 assigned units. Not counting an outlier from this group, which was eliminated in the diagnosis, the $n = 106$ units were reassigned as follows: $n = 21$ in group 1, $n = 4$ in group 2, $n = 0$ in group 3, $n = 8$ in group 4, $n = 1$ in group 5, $n = 3$ in group 6, $n = 64$ in group 7, and $n = 5$ in group 8. In group BC, the authors assigned $n = 125$ units; in the new classification, of these, $n = 5$ were assigned to group 1, $n = 5$ to group 2, $n = 0$ to group 3, $n = 99$ to group 4, $n = 1$ to group 5, $n = 7$ to group 6, $n = 6$ to group 7, and $n = 2$ to group 8. And so on with the rest of the groups.

With these results, it can be concluded that applying PCA and the Mahalanobis distance to assign samples to groups presents serious problems, since it uses a matrix of covariances with contaminated data; if the sample size of the groups is small compared with the size of the p-variables, the inversion of the covariance matrices can become a problem and lead to singular matrices. In

Table 5 Sample assignment to $K = 8$ groups using variable selection and projection-based clustering for data from Harry, Fish, and Fish (2002)

Groups	A	BC	E	F	G	South Tucson	Phoenix	Papagueria	Assigned by SelvarMix	Total samples by group with variable selection
Group 1	21	5	17	2	23	0	0	1	48	117
Group 2	4	5	7	3	1	19	0	0	69	107
Group 3	0	0	0	0	0	1	11	25	3	40
Group 4	8	99	0	0	3	1	0	0	27	138
Group 5	1	1	1	11	2	1	0	0	35	52
Group 6	3	7	1	1	4	0	0	0	62	78
Group 7	64	6	3	2	2	0	0	0	23	100
Group 8	5	2	3	1	4	1	0	0	61	77
Total samples by group	106	125	32	20	39	23	11	26	327	710

addition, if the assumption of normality is violated, there is a risk of over-representing some of the K groups while others may be underrepresented. It is clear that, to achieve a good segmentation of the groups, it is necessary to include in the analysis a procedure that, although more elaborate, can discover the trend of the data in their characteristic groups.

10 Compositional Study of Obsidian Materials: Example of Semi-Supervised Classification

Now suppose that you need to correctly assign obsidian artifacts collected from archaeological sites to their respective raw material deposits. Reviewing published studies on provenance analysis, it is common to see overlaps between sources and the impossibility of their statistical methods to discriminate between sub-sources. One available example of this can be found in Glascock et al. (1998), who used NAA to analyze obsidian samples from nine geographical regions from Central Mexico and Guatemala. The region of Guatemala involved all the sources and sub-sources of the highlands, including El Chayal, Ixtepeque, and San Martin Jilotepeque, as well as other less important sources. For Mexico, the sources and sub-sources included Otumba Malpaís, Pico de Orizaba, Pachuca, Paredon, Tulancingo, Ucareo, Zacualtipan, and Zaragoza. Using 21 components, transforming the data to $\log_{10}$, analyzing the data with PCA, and projecting the first two components, overlaps were obtained between all the deposits in Guatemala and the Otumba deposit, and it was not possible to differentiate the sub-sources of any of the deposits. From an archaeological point of view, this would be a big miscalculation, since sites that are hundreds or thousands of kilometers apart should not overlap, and the inferences derived from artifacts that come from sources 1,000 km apart can be very different.

However, not being able to differentiate sub-sources limits the interpretation of the patterns of exploitation of raw materials. Therefore, the procedure must be corrected in order to obtain well-separated groups and avoid errors in the assignments. When partially labeled data are used, the labeled data should be considered error-free. In other words, there should be certainty of the provenance of the geological samples, whether they come from a primary source (collected directly from volcanic flow) or secondary source (product of erosion and dragging), or even distinguishing between individual sources (a single volcanic event) or sub-sources (product of more than one volcanic event) either by geological or geochemical studies. For instance, when there are obsidian sources that have multiple related chemical signatures but that are geochemically differentiable, these can be considered as sub-sources. El Chayal, Pachuca, and Oyameles are examples of regions that underwent various volcanic events that allowed the formation of more than one obsidian flow, which are geochemically differentiable.

Therefore, distinguishing sub-sources may be essential to understand differences in exploitation patterns in space or time (Dolan, 2016). Another problem is that, despite the large number of obsidian sources known in the North American southwest, northern Mexico, central Mexico, and Central America, few studies publish the complete compositional dataset of the sites for anyone to be able to work statistically with them and compare the samples recovered at archaeological sites to determine their provenance. Commonly, authors only publish a single data value per natural deposit, specifying only the average, the standard deviation, and the minimum and maximum values; this information is not enough for working with more advanced statistical methods or computing results with a higher degree of certainty. For the case of obsidian, some exceptions are found in Argote Espino et al. (2012), Carr (2015), Dolan et al. (2017), López-García et al. (2024), Millhauser et al. (2015), and Pierce (2015); currently, MURR Archaeometry Laboratory makes its databases available to people who personally request them.

To exemplify the semi-supervised classification method useful to solve cases where there are controlled samples from raw material deposits and archaeological materials whose origin is not known, we decided to use the geochemical data of obsidian sources collected and published by Shackley (2005). Steven Shackley has extensively researched obsidians from the North American southwest and has made his data available online to other researchers (see www.swxrflab.net/swobsrcs.htm). In this exercise, it was decided to look for deposits that had the largest number of components registered in order to manage the greater variability in each of them. The four deposits that were not included in the exercise were the following:

- Mule Creek complex, in western New Mexico, since only seven components (Ma, Rb, Sr, Y, Zr, Nb, and Ba) were registered.
- Gwynn and Ewe Canyons (Negro Mountain), west of New Mexico, where up to 10 components are published, but a large number of samples did not present values for some components such as Zn, Pb, and Th.
- Red Hill field, western New Mexico, where there were a great many missing values for Ba.

In this way, all those deposits that had at least 10 registered components, the least number of missing values, and a large enough sample size were selected. Considering these three conditions, it was possible to form a matrix including 12 deposits (Table 6); the retained components were Ti, Mn, Fe, Zn, Rb, Sr, Y, Zr, Nb, and Ba. The resulting matrix consisted of $n = 400$ observations and $D = 10$

Table 6 Name and number of samples from obsidian deposits in the North American southwest included in the semi-supervised clustering. Modified from the original data source in Shackley (2005).

Source name	n
Sandtanks	43
Topaz Basin	45
Vulture	29
Picketpost Mountain	51
111 Ranch Form	22
Cow Canyon Prim	41
MCDaniel Tank Rhyolite	19
La Jara Mesa	53
Grants Ridge	25
Canovas Canyon Rhyolite	38
North Dome	14
East Side	20
Total samples analyzed	**400**

parts; to follow this exercise, the matrix is provided as file "Ex2_NMObsidian.csv" in the Supplementary Material. Since some samples presented values < LOD, these were imputed using the **MICE** algorithm, which also allows the visual comparison of the data pattern after imputation with the data pattern with no imputation. If the imputation is reliable, the pattern of the unimputed values (dark gray dots) will follow the same trend as the pattern of the imputed values (light gray dots). In Figure 10 it can be seen that the only components with missing values are Ti, Zn, and Ba and that the trend of dark gray and light gray dots is the same.

After imputation, a diagnosis of the data was made with the ROBPCA algorithm, which did not detect any outliers in the matrix. Later, to properly compare the results obtained with semi-supervised clustering versus traditional methods, the same matrix was processed both ways. First, PCA was carried out following the MURR methodology (Glascock et al., 1998), transforming the data into $\log_{10}$ and plotting the first two PCs. In Figure 11, although there is a group structure with a maximum of eight groups, some peripheral points can be visually perceived. If the data are labeled by their reference site and a probability ellipse of 95% is plotted (Figure 12), overlaps

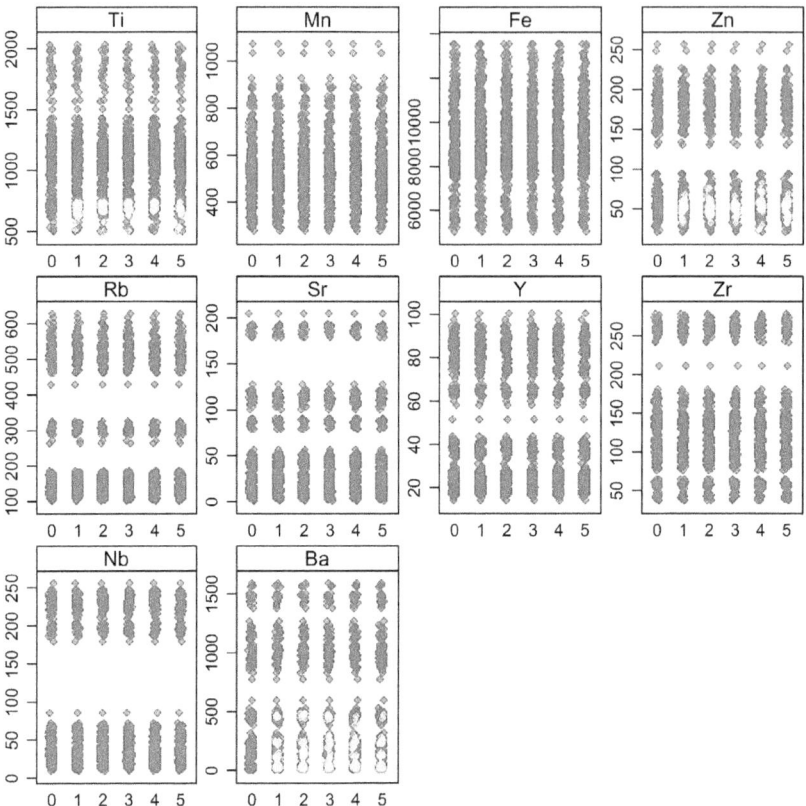

Figure 10 Strip plot of the ten variables (components) in the original and imputed datasets. The dark gray dots represent the unimputed values, and the light gray dots represent the imputed values.

between Cow Canyon Prim and Ranch Form, Grants Ridge and La Jara Mesa, and Vulture and Canovas Canyon Rhyolite are observed, and it is difficult to differentiate between North Dome, Picketpost Mountain and Topaz Basin. This is even though the variability explained by the model is 87.80%. With this simple example we can see that PCA is not a very suitable technique to distinguish between different sources.

Next, a semi-supervised classification was conducted. For that purpose, we recommend using either of two R packages: **Rmixmod**, which allows partial labeling of all algorithms (unsupervised, semi-supervised, and supervised), or **upclass** (Russell et al., 2013), which is a complementary package to the **mclust** package and with which we have had very good results when applying it to partially labeled data (López-García et al., 2024). For our analysis, first, the data were transformed into the isometric log ratio. Subsequently, an

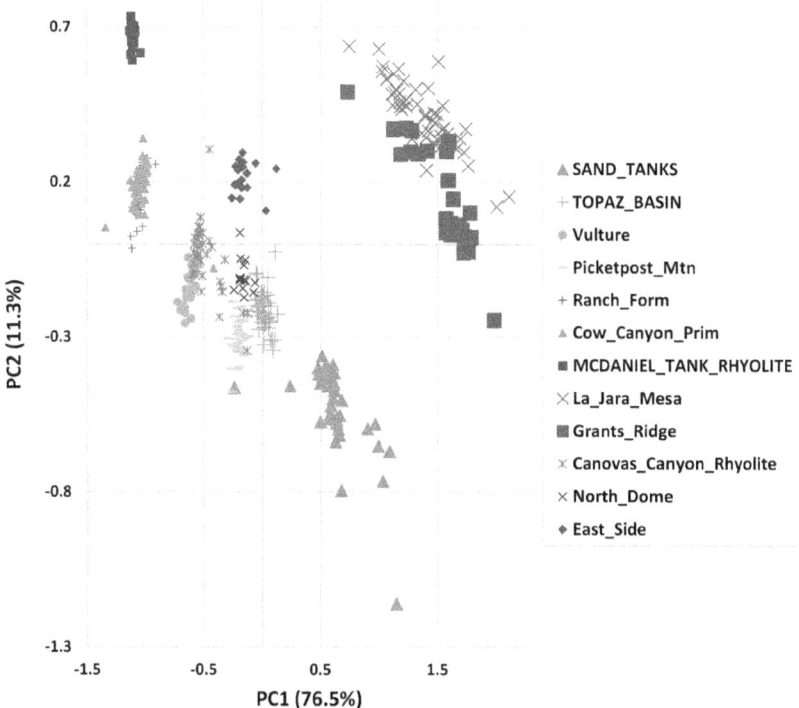

Figure 11 Scatterplot of the principal component analysis of the obsidian sources from the North American southwest. Modified from the original data Source in Shackley (2005). Color version available at www.cambridge.org/determining-provenance

experiment was designed where a sample was randomly extracted from the dataset, and the provenance of the rest was predicted. That is, the dataset x was divided into two subsets, one of them with the individuals with known labels z_i and the other with the unlabeled individuals ("unknown" labels). To follow this exercise, the data matrices are provided in the Supplementary Material as files "Ex2_Known_samples.csv" and "Ex2_Unknown_samples.csv."

Using **Rmixmod**, semi-supervised classification was performed using the functions mixmodCluster(), mixmodLearn() and mixmodPredict(). The mixmodCluster function allows the user to provide known tags for some of the observations; in this, the knownLabels argument corresponds to a numerical vector of size n that contains the known labels z, where each individual sample or specimen registers its own label related to its deposit provenance. For this step, in our case we established the parameter 'family = "all"' to adjust a total of

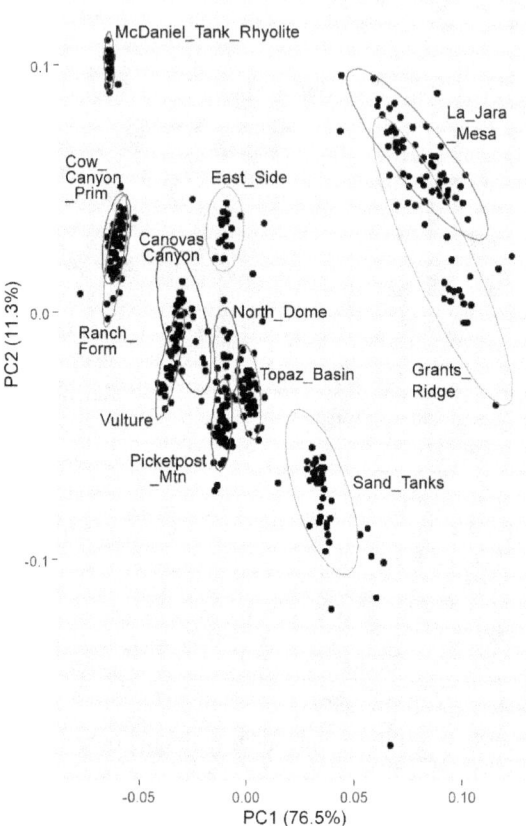

Figure 12 Scatterplot of the principal component analysis of the obsidian sources from the North American southwest with a probability ellipse of 95%. Original data source in Shackley (2005). Color version available at www.cambridge.org/determining-provenance

28 models using the BIC and CV criteria and select the best model in terms of fitness, data complexity, and group separability (Langrognet et al., 2025). With the training observations, mixmodLearn() calculates the first step of the DA, finding the best classification rule by executing step M of the maximum likelihood algorithm found in the EM algorithm. The mixmodLearn() function returns an instance of the class with the same name, MixmodLearn, containing two attributes: "results," showing all the results obtained in ascending order according to the BIC criterion, and 'bestResults,' showing the selection of the model that best fits the data. The mixmodPredict() function only needs two arguments: a data matrix of the remaining observations (observations with no

Table 7 Number of samples per source used for the learning process and the prediction of the semi-supervised classifier

ID no.	Source	n	Learning samples	Unlabeled samples
1	Sand tanks	43	19	24
2	Topaz Basin	45	17	28
3	Vulture	29	14	15
4	Picketpost Mountain	51	26	25
5	111 Ranch Form	22	8	14
6	Cow Canyon Prim	41	17	24
7	MCDaniel Tank Rhyolite	19	10	9
8	La Jara Mesa	53	27	26
9	Grants Ridge	25	10	15
10	Canovas Canyon Rhyolite	38	19	19
11	North Dome	14	3	11
12	East Side	20	10	10
	TOTAL	**400**	**180**	**220**

labels) and a classification rule, which is estimated by the algorithm in the previous step (Lebret et al., 2015).

In the prediction, the algorithm is instructed to use in the classification rule for the model that obtained the best result. The instance of the MixmodPredict class contains the predicted partitions and probabilities for the assignation of the unlabeled observations to the K groups. In this example, the entire dataset was first divided into a learning set of $n = 180$ (equivalent to 45% of the observations) and a test set with the remaining 220 observations. Table 7 shows the number of samples used for each of the sources; the "Learning Samples" column corresponds to the number of samples randomly extracted to train the classifier ($n = 180$). The model that best fitted the data was *Gaussian_pK_Lk_Bk*, which corresponds to the general family with equal volume, equal shape, and equal orientation. In the next step, the prediction is made; here, we indicate to the semi-supervised classifier that 55% of the labels are unknown and that it must predict which group they belong to.

Table 8 presents the results of the semi-supervised classification. With the help of the unlabeled data, only eight sorting errors occur, which correspond to the boxes marked in gray in the table; the rest were correctly assigned to their respective group. In other words, all the samples that appear in the main

Table 8 Prediction of unlabeled samples to their respective groups

Canovas Canyon Rhyolite	Cow Canyon Prim	East Side	Grants Ridge	La Jara Mesa	McDaniel Tank Rhyolite	North Dome	Picketpost Mountain	111 Ranch Form	Sand Tanks	Topaz Basin	Vulture	Total
19	0	0	0	0	0	0	0	0	0	0	0	19
0	**21**	0	0	0	0	0	0	3	0	0	0	24
0	0	**10**	0	0	0	0	0	0	0	0	0	10
0	0	0	**15**	0	0	0	0	0	0	0	0	15
0	0	0	3	**23**	0	0	0	0	0	0	0	26
0	0	0	0	0	**9**	0	0	0	0	0	0	9
0	0	0	0	0	0	**11**	0	0	0	0	0	11
0	0	0	0	0	0	0	**25**	0	0	0	0	25
0	2	0	0	0	0	0	0	**12**	0	0	0	14
0	0	0	0	0	0	0	0	0	**24**	0	0	24
0	0	0	0	0	0	0	0	0	0	**28**	0	28
0	0	0	0	0	0	0	0	0	0	0	**15**	15
19	23	10	18	23	9	11	25	15	24	28	15	220

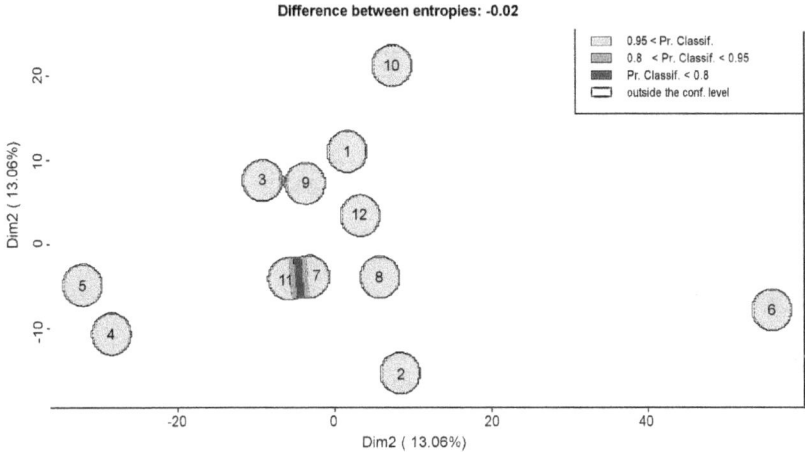

Figure 13 Component interpretation graph of the samples from the North American southwest. (Original databases from Shackley, 2005.)

diagonal of Table 8 were correctly assigned to their deposits of origin; the samples outside the main diagonal correspond to classification error, this error being only 2.27%. Figure 13 shows the bivariate spherical Gaussian visualization, where it is easy to observe that the 12 sources have a good separation and where the difference between entropies, which evaluates the quality of the Gaussian visualization compared to the original groups (Biernacki et al., 2021), is small $\hat{\delta fg}$ = (-0.02); as explained in Section 7.1, a difference between entropies close to 0 means that the representation is accurate, therefore indicating the good precision of the model. The sum of the inertia of the first two axes is 58.91% + 13.06% = 71.96% of the discriminant power; therefore, it can be stated that most of the discriminant information is present in this two-dimensional mapping. In addition, each group is represented by its center and has a 95% confidence level border; this result indicates a good correspondence between the two mapping spaces: the native space of the MBC and the Gaussian spherical space of visualization.

Although there appears to be an overlap between components 1 and 7 (which correspond to the Sand Tanks and McDaniel Tank Rhyolite deposits), this does not mean that the samples from these sites are assigned to groups that do not correspond to them but rather indicates that the covariance matrices of their components are somewhat similar. As part of the output, the 'results' attribute gives information to the user about the partition of the mixture model and the probabilities of belonging to the groups, where the samples of each of these components are classified as separate groups. In the graph, it can also be seen

Table 9 Number of samples per source used in the second example for the learning process and the prediction of the semi-supervised classifier

ID no.	Source	Learning samples	Unlabeled samples	Correctly assigned
1	Sand tanks	19	24	24
2	Topaz Basin	13	32	32
3	Vulture	12	17	17
4	Picketpost Mountain	16	35	35
5	111 Ranch Form	8	14	14
6	Cow Canyon Prim	15	26	26
7	MCDaniel Tank Rhyolite	8	11	11
8	La Jara Mesa	15	38	38
9	Grants Ridge	12	13	13
10	Canovas Canyon Rhyolite	14	24	24
11	North Dome	7	7	7
12	East Side	10	10	10
	Total	149	251	251

that the components with the greatest chemical variability with respect to the rest of the deposits are 10, 6, 2, 5, and 4, as shown by their position at the extremes of the graph; these correspond to the Canovas Canyon Rhyolite, Cow Canyon Prim, Topaz Basin, Ranch Form, and Picketpost Mountain sites.

If you have a set of labeled samples (e.g., natural sources) and a new set of unlabeled samples (e.g., artifacts) and your aim is to predict to which group each of samples of unknown origin belong, you can use the **Rmixmod** package to enhance the effect of predicting new observations. To exemplify this, we decided to divide the database into two subsets, the first now with $n = 149$ labeled samples and the second with $n = 251$ unlabeled samples. In the first column of Table 9, you can see the number of labeled samples for each of the deposits and, in the second column, the number of unlabeled samples. In this case, as the label of the known samples is multinomial, it is considered a heterogeneous data model from which an object of the class CompositeModel is generated. This contains some of the 40 heterogeneous models to fit in **Rmixmod** and incorporates the arguments 'free. proportions (FALSE or TRUE)' to include models with free proportions, as well as 'equal.proportions (FALSE or TRUE)' to include models with equal or variable proportions (Langrognet et al., 2025).

Running the model with the data in the example, of the 40 models calculated, the one that best fits the data is "Heterogeneous_p_E_L_B," which detects groups with volume = free and shape = equal. The third column of Table 9 refers to the assignment made by the model, where the samples are assigned to their respective deposit with an accuracy of 100%. This exercise allowed us to show that semi-supervised classification, using limited monitoring of the data, improves the results of clustering. The **Rmixmod** package, due to its flexibility, allows the adjustment of a large family of models, from which the best one can be selected considering datasets of arbitrary shapes and sizes.

11 Final Comments

Conventional methodologies used for provenance analyses of archaeological materials have several drawbacks as they do not consider the intrinsic nature of compositional data. When working with numerical data, a common question is how the data should be preprocessed before clustering or classification (e.g., data transformation, outlier diagnosis, variable selection, model selection). If proper preprocessing is not performed, chemical data can contribute to noise and negatively affect the results of a classification. A review of the existing literature on provenance analysis showed that a large number of studies present only exploratory results that are not validated and where overlaps between groups predominate.

If the goal of clustering or classification is to discover significant clusters in the data and to confidently assess the membership of samples in each of the clusters, it would be expected that in provenance studies the clusters would be compact and well separated and that there would be no overlap between the clusters, unless the chemical groups shared common elements. However, when using these procedures as they have traditionally been conducted, uncertainty will always be present in the analysis. Many of the classification problems are due to the violation of the theoretical assumptions of classical statistical techniques. For example, although the first components of the PCA explain the greatest amount of variation, if the correlation between the variables is not linear, its use as a method for the discovery of groups turns out to be ineffective. In addition, classical methods are not robust in the presence of outliers, so an adequate diagnosis of the data turns out to be an indispensable task to avoid introducing biases in the matrices of variances and covariances and in the location vectors.

Another recurring problem in chemical analyses is the elimination of samples for registering values < LOD. This procedure must be questioned since, on the one hand, it removes important information that could alter the data analysis by reducing the size of the samples and, on the other, there is a risk of eliminating variables that are necessary in for analysis, which results in a distortion of the real results. Thus, data imputation should be considered part of the research process if the intention is to draw meaningful conclusions in the presence of solid empirical evidence. The advantages of imputation procedures should not be gauged by the mere fact that they allow information to be replaced to fit models and test hypotheses, but by the fact that, if the imputation is done correctly, the estimators will be close to the true value of the population parameter.

It was possible to detect that the procedures for selecting relevant variables in high-dimensional spaces are not considered, even though it has been shown that including all variables can result in the masking of the groups. Including all variables simultaneously can have negative effects on the search for groups due to the redundancy of information and the presence of noise produced by the irrelevant variables. This is why we argue that, when using high-dimensional spaces such as data obtained with NAA instruments, variable selection should be part of the classification procedure. Through model-based variable selection methods, it was possible to prove that, of the total set of variables, only a subset of these contains relevant information for clustering purposes. Thus, the inclusion of a large number of variables that do not have group information tends to over-fit the model, causing greater difficulty in defining the structure of the results.

Another issue is that different materials lead to different problems that need to be solved. For example, analyzing ceramic data is a more complex task than analyzing obsidians, since their composition is more heterogeneous thanks to the varied ingredients and the different recipes used in the manufacture of the pieces. That is why variable selection must be applied to each database separately to figure out which variables are more significant for the study; selecting variables arbitrarily before classification can cause important clustering information to be lost, including the risk of omitting important variables and of including redundant variables. In addition, some variables may have significant information about clustering when used in combination with other variables, but not in isolation (Murphy, Dean & Raftery, 2010). It cannot be assumed that, just because in one study a certain number of variables were selected with successful results, these same variables will be successful in other studies, yielding the same results. That is why bivariate deployments must be debated, since they do not have any formal statistical support beyond the personal experience of individual researchers.

In provenance studies, there are usually large gaps in the corroboration of the results, since statistical validation processes are often not implemented to confirm whether the procedure and results are correct and, therefore, whether the inferences are sound with respect to the behavior of the data. After a provenance analysis, it is essential to validate the results of a clustering or classification algorithm, which can be evaluated based on statistical criteria such as indices. These allow you to determine the clustering trend and check if there is a nonrandom structure in the data, as well as evaluate how well the results fit the model. Without proper validation of the results, it is not possible to be certain whether the clustering algorithm is the right one for the data in question, whether the number of clusters is optimal, or whether the elements of the sample were correctly assigned.

For the reasons stated, in this Element we have mainly addressed the problem of the provenance of archaeological materials, reformulating and updating the statistical procedures conventionally used to achieve the correct assignment of experimental units with their respective sites; that is, of the sources of raw material that were exploited to create the artifacts that we find in more distant places. In the proposed step-by-step methodology, the preprocessing methods were discussed, which are an inherent part of knowledge discovery in database processing (Zaki & Meira, 2014). They serve to manage data cleansing, integration, transformation, and reduction for the next phase of clustering and classification. During this phase, it was possible to prove that the correct transformation of data can improve the performance of the models.

Data diagnostics were included to detect and eliminate outliers, along with methods for the selection of informative variables, which offer information on which variables are significant for classification purposes. It was also shown that the inclusion of noisy or uninformative variables can mask the underlying clustering structures of the data. In this way, it was possible to observe that preprocessing is as important as the clustering algorithms and, therefore, it is worth emphasizing that all these steps are closely interrelated. As a solution to evaluate the provenance of unlabeled observations, model-based semi-supervised classification was proposed, providing information on the group membership of the observations and achieving more reliable results. The conditional probabilities of group membership are determined on the basis of Gaussian mixture models as a clustering method, using the maximum likelihood estimation and expressing the a posteriori maximum rule; this is a probabilistic framework for solving the problem of density estimation that provides a classification with a minimal probability of error.

With the implemented procedure, it is possible to detect natural groups through the modeling of flexible covariance structures by defining groups with different sizes, shapes, and volumes. This method allows the use of well-established statistical principles to be established in the estimation of parameters and in the selection and evaluation of models. The main advantage of these procedures is that they are formulated as a probabilistic model selection process where it is possible to evaluate uncertainty more rigorously. Other advantages are the simultaneous clustering of high-dimensional data, selecting informative variables, and determining the optimal number of groups. In this way, semi-supervised clustering allows for better clustering than that obtained from unlabeled data alone or from supervised classification.

Unlike traditional multivariate techniques that only allow one model to be tested on the data, such as PCA, LDA, and cluster analysis, with MBC it is possible to test m candidate models to find the best fit for the data. This produces better performance in the classification of archaeological materials, showing consistency in the selection of the model and the number of clusters. As for validating the clustering solution, emphasis is placed on using robust visualization procedures that allow the quality of the groups and their separation, distribution, and shape to be appreciated. Finally, we illustrated several advantages of using Gaussian mixture models in conjunction with properly defined transformations to identify homogeneous groups of data from their chemical components, using examples of ceramic and obsidian materials analyzed with instruments such as NAA and XRF. We hope that the methodology proposed in this Element will be useful for those who wish to determine the origin of their ancient artifacts in a more scientific, objective, and reliable way.

Appendix: Scripts for R

Important note: Considering the first example of the ceramic samples, use the array (matrix) with 32 components (variables) and 720 samples; the header (name of the variables) is in the first row and the labels (name of the samples) are in the first column. Suppose your array file is named "Pottery.csv" and it is in a folder in the root directory (e.g., C:\\Ceramic\\).

Value Imputation with the MICE Package

```
rm(list = ls())
setwd("C:\\other_directory") ## Change the path to the directory where the array is located
## Multivariate Imputation by Chained Equations
library(mice) ## (van Buuren & Groothuis-Oudshoorn, 2011)
## In the input matrix, the values to be imputed must be labeled as NA
data <- read.csv("C:\\Ceramic\\Pottery.csv",header=T)
str(data)
data2 <- data[,2:33] ## Works only with components without the labels of the first column
str(data2)
imputed_Data <- mice(data2, m=5, maxit = 50, method = "pmm", seed = 500)
summary(imputed_Data)
str(imputed_Data)
imputed_Data$imp$Ba
completeData2 <- complete(imputed_Data,5)
Write.csv(completeData2,file="Pottery_imputed.csv") ## Writes the name of the file
```

Value Imputation with the zCompositions Package

```
rm(list=ls())
## Treatment of Zeros, and Left-Censored Data, and Missing Values in Compositional Datasets
library(zCompositions) ## (Palarea-Albaladejo & Martín-Fernández, 2015)
## The values to be imputed must be labeled as 0
data <- read.csv("C:\\Ceramic\\Pottery.csv", header=T)
str(data)
data2 <- data[,2:33] # Eliminates identification variables
```

```
str(data2)       # See the structure of the data
LPdata2_lrDAmiss <- lrDA(data2,label=0,imp.missing=TRUE,
closure=10^6)
Write.csv(LPdata2_lrDAmiss, file="Pottery_left_cens_imputed.
csv") ## Writes file name
```

Log Ratio Transformations

```
## Centered Log Ratio (clr) and Isometric (ilr) Transformation
## Suppose that you don´t need to impute values and the array is
still named Pottery.csv
library(compositions)  ## (van den Boogaart, Tolosana-Delgado,
& Bren, 2023)
setwd("C:\other_directory")  ## Change the path to the direc-
tory where the array is located
list.files() ## List out every file in a specific folder. The array
must have a .csv extension.
Data <- read.csv ("C:\\Ceramic\\Pottery.csv", header=T)
## read the file with the raw data
str(Data)      ## See the data structure
Data1 <- Data [, 2: 33]       # Removes the first column with the
labels from the data; be careful to
## Change the last number according to the number of considered
components (# last column)
Data1 <- acomp(Data)     ## Apply closure operator
Data2 <- clr(Data1)    ## Transforms the data to centered log ratio
Data3 <- ilr(Data1)    ## Transforms the data to isometric log ratio
Write.csv(Data2, file="Pottery_clr.csv")     # Save the file with
the clr transformation
Write.csv(Data3, file="Pottery_ilr.csv")     # Save the file with
the ilr transformation; note
## that the resulting file will have the number of original
components – 1.
```

Detection of Outliers

```
rm (list=ls())
library(robustbase) ## (Maechler, 2023)
data <-
read.csv("C:\\Ceramic\\Pottery_ilr.csv",header=T) ## Calls
the transformed file
str(data)
```

```
data2 <- data[,2:33]    ## The last number corresponds to the
number of columns
## (components+1)
str(data2)
ao.hbk <- adjOutlyingness(data2)
str(ao.hbk)
hist(ao.hbk $adjout)    ## Really two groups
table(ao.hbk$nonOut) ## Tells you the no. of outliers and the no.
of non-outliers
## To tell you which are the outliers:
which(!ao.hbk$nonOut)     #1..14 - but not for all random seeds!
## Manually remove the detected outliers from your transformed
array (ilr or clr), and give
## the file another name (e.g., "File_X.csv")
```

Selection of Variables with the Clustvarsel Package

```
## Variable Selection Methodology for Gaussian Model-Based
Clustering
## Gaussian finite mixture model fitted by EM algorithm
## The following code uses the backward/forward greedy search
for variable
## selection, which by default is performed over all the covari-
ance decomposition models
## and numbers of mixture components from 2 up to 9:
rm(list = ls())
library(clustvarsel) # (Scrucca & Raftery, 2018)
help(package="clustvarsel")
X <- read.csv("C:\\Ceramic\\File_X.csv", header=T) ## Reads
the file with the array after
# removing the outliers, if any were found; if not, use your
transformed file (e.g., ilr).
str(X)
X1 <- X[,2:33] ### The last number corresponds to the number of
columns (components)
str(X1)
out <- clustvarsel(X, G = 2:9) # Stepwise (forward/backward)
greedy search
out
summary(out)
str(out)
out$model$classification
```

Selection of Variables with the SelvarMix Package

```
library (SelvarMix) ### (Sedki, Celeux, & Maugis-Rabusseau, 2017)
rm(list = ls())
dat <- read.csv("C:\\Ceramic\\File_X.csv", header=T) ## Reads the file with the array after
# removing the outliers, if any were found; if not, use your transformed file (ilr or clr)
str(dat)
set.seed(123)
mixmodGaussianModel(
family = "all", ## The function family can be "spherical," "general," or "all"
listModels = NULL,
free.proportions = TRUE,
equal.proportions = TRUE)
obj <- SelvarClustLasso(x=dat, nbcluster=2:9, models=mixmodGaussianModel())
summary(obj)
print(obj)
obj$partition      # Returns the assignations predicted by the best model
obj$nbcluster
obj$model
obj$parameters
```

Selection of Variables with the VarSelLCM Package

```
rm(list=ls())
library(VarSelLCM) # Marbac, M. and Sedki, M. (2017)
data <- read.csv("\\Ceramic\\File_X.csv", header=T) ## Reads the file with the array after
# removing the outliers, if any were found; if not, use your transformed file (ilr or clr)
str(data)
sel_with <- VarSelCluster(data, gvals = 2:9, nbcores = 2, initModel=40, crit.varsel = "MICL")
fitted(sel_with)
plot(sel_with, type="probs-class")
summary(sel_with)
plot(sel_with)
VarSelShiny(sel_with) # Returns the most relevant variables
```

Silhouette Plot with the Cluster Package

```
# Create a new file leaving only the components selected by the
best model (in our example SelvarMix). Give it a different name
(e.g., File_X_Selvarmix.csv)
library(cluster) ## (Maechler, Rousseeuw, Struyf, Hubert, &
Hornik, 2024)
rm(list = ls())
data1 <- read.csv("C:\\Ceramic\\File_X_Selvarmix.csv",
header=T)
str(data1)
data3 <- data1[,1:17] ## Removes the first column with the ID of
the data, considering the
# 17 components selected by SelvarMix (best model)
str(data3)
pr4 <- pam(data3, 8) ## For evaluating a maximum of eight groups
str(si <- silhouette(pr4))
(ssi <- summary(si))
plot(si) # silhouette plot
plot(si, col = c("red", "green", "blue", "purple", "forest
green", "dark blue", "purple2", "goldenrod4")) # with cluster-
wise coloring
```

Robust Clustering Data Projection with the Databionic Swarm Package

```
## To run the DatabionicSwarm package, it is important to load
the packages rlang, shiny, ## Umatrix,
ProjectionBasedClustering, GeneralizadUmatix, and ggplot2.
rm(list=ls())
library(DatabionicSwarm)
Data <- read.csv("C:\\Ceramic\\File_X_Selvarmix", header=T)
str(Data)
InputDistances = as.matrix(dist(Data))
projection = Pswarm(InputDistances,
    Cls = Data$Cls,
    PlotIt = T,
    Silent = T)
library(DatabionicSwarm)
library(GeneralizedUmatrix)
visualization = GeneratePswarmVisualization(
Data = InputDistances,
```

```
projection$ProjectedPoints,
projection$LC)
GeneralizedUmatrix::plotTopographicMap(
visualization$Umatrix,
visualization$Bestmatches)
library(DatabionicSwarm)
library(GeneralizedUmatrix)
Cls = DBSclustering(StructureType = FALSE,
k = 8, ## Specify the number of clusters determined by the best
model; see "obj$partition"
InputDistances,
visualization$Bestmatches,
visualization$LC,
PlotIt = FALSE)
GeneralizedUmatrix::plotTopographicMap(
visualization$Umatrix,
visualization$Bestmatches,
BmSize=0.65, # This command is used to change the size of the data
points on the topographic map
Cls)
ClusteringAccuracy(Data$Cls,Cls)

#Generating the Shape of an Island out of the Topograpahic Map
library(DatabionicSwarm)
library(ProjectionBasedClustering)
library(GeneralizedUmatrix)
Imx = ProjectionBasedClustering::
interactiveGeneralizedUmatrixIsland(
visualization$Umatrix,
visualization$Bestmatches,
Cls)

GeneralizedUmatrix::plotTopographicMap(
visualization$Umatrix,
visualization$Bestmatches,
BmSize=0.75, # This command is used to change the size of the data
points on the
#topographic map
Cls = Cls,
Imx = Imx)

#Manually Improving the Clustering Using the Topograpahic Map
library(ProjectionBasedClustering)
```

Appendix: Scripts for R

```
Cls2 = ProjectionBasedClustering::interactiveClustering(
visualization$Umatrix,
visualization$Bestmatches,
Cls)

library(DataVisualizations) #(Thrun & Ultsch, 2021)
Heatmap(as.matrix(dist(Data)),Cls = Cls)
Silhouetteplot(Data,Cls =Cls)
```

Important note on the method used in the obsidian example: To follow the exercise in Section 10 of this Element, see file "Ex2_NMObsidian.csv" in the Supplementary Material containing the matrix with 400 samples and 10 components of the data extracted from M. Steven Shackley's web page <http://www.swxrflab.net/swobsrcs.htm>.

Semi-Supervised Classification with the Rmixmod Package

```
# Apply this script as if you had already applied the first three
steps of the preprocessing
# (imputation, transformation, and diagnosis) to the original
matrix, and your new
#matrix is now called "ilr_imputed.csv." The header is the first
row, and the sample IDs are
#in the first column.
rm(list = ls())
setwd("C:\\")         ## Change the path to the directory where
your array is located
library(Rmixmod)
data <-read.csv("C:\\ilr_imputed.csv",header=T) ## Reads the
file
str(data)
sel = sample(nrow(data),180) ## Start by extracting randomly
180 observations from the dataset as the training set
sel      ## Displays selected observations
X = data[sel,1:9]; labels = X.labels = data$Source[sel]
#Assuming that the name of the
## Samples are in the first column, and you have nine components
(variables), since you
#employed the ilr transformation (with D-1)
labels
Y = data[-sel, 1:9]; Y.labels = data$Source[-sel] ##
Observations selected to label. Assuming
## that the sample names are in the first column and you have nine
components.
```

```
Y
per = 0.80 # Percentage of unlabeled data
labels[1: round(per*nrow(X))] = NA
labels
per
strategy2 <- mixmodStrategy (algo=c("SEM","EM"),
initMethod ="CEM",nbIterationInAlgo=c(200,100),
epsilonInAlgo=c(NA,0.0001))
model = mixmodGaussianModel(
family = "all",
listModels = NULL,
free.proportions = TRUE,
equal.proportions = FALSE
)
res1 = mixmodCluster(X,12,knownLabels=X.labels,models=mo-
del,strategy=strategy2)
table(mixmodPredict(Y,res1@bestResult)@partition,
Y.labels)
str(res1)
res1@bestResult@partition
res1@bestResult
library(ClusVis)
resvisu <- clusvisMixmod(res1)
plotDensityClusVisu(resvisu, add.obs = F, positionlegend =
"bottomright")library(ClusVis)
resvisu <- clusvisMixmod(res1)
plotDensityClusVisu(resvisu, add.obs = F, positionlegend =
"bottomright")
```

Predicting Samples to Known Groups Using the Rmixmod Package

```
## Create two files, one with the 180 labeled samples (labels are
in the first column) and
## one with 220 unlabeled samples (sample names are in the first
column) and provide
## different names for both files with the header in the first row.
In our case, we called
## them "Ex2_Unknown_samples.csv" and "Ex2_Known_samples.
csv."
rm(list = ls())
library(Rmixmod)
datax <- read.csv("C:\\Ex2_Known_samples", header=T) # File
```

Appendix: Scripts for R

```
with sample tags
str(datax)
dataz <- read.csv("C:\\Ex2_Unknown_samples", header=T) #
Untagged samples
str(dataz)
dataz1 <- dataz[,2:9] ## Removes the labeled column from the data
str(dataz1)
model = mixmodGaussianModel()
datax$Source
##CompositeModel
## Define a list of heterogeneous models to test in MIXMOD
model = mixmodCompositeModel(
listModels = NULL,
free.proportions = TRUE,
equal.proportions = FALSE,
variable.independency = NULL,
component.independency = NULL
)
## Then we run a mixmodLearn() analysis without those 180 labeled
observations
learn <- mixmodLearn(datax,datax$Source, models = model)
str(learn)
## Create a MixmodPredict to predict those 220 unlabeled obser-
vations
prediction <- mixmodPredict(dataz, classificationRule=learn
["bestResult"])
# Show results
summary(prediction)
prediction
prediction@partition
learn["bestResult"]
plot(learn, showOnly ="quantitative",c(1,2))
```

References

Adolfsson, A., Ackerman, M., & Brownstein, N. (2019). To cluster, or not to cluster: An analysis of clusterability methods. *Pattern Recognition*, *88*, 13–26.

Aitchison, J. (1986). *The statistical analysis of compositional data*. London: Chapman & Hall.

Aitchison, J. (2003). A concise guide to compositional data analysis. *2nd Compositional Data Analysis Workshop* (pp. 1–134). Girona, Spain: Universitat de Girona.

Alelyani, S., Tang, J., & Liu, H. (2014). Feature selection for clustering: A review. In C. Aggarwal & C. Reddy (eds.), *Data clustering: Algorithms and applications* (pp. 1–32). Hoboken: Chapman and Hall/CRC Press.

Ambrose, W., Allen, C., O'Connor, S., Spriggs, M., Vasco Oliveira, N., & Reepmeyer, C. (2009). Possible obsidian sources for artifacts from Timor: Narrowing the options using chemical data. *Journal of Archaeological Science*, *36*(*3*), 607–615.

Andrews, J. & McNicholas, P. (2014). Variable selection for clustering and classification. *Journal of Classification*, *31*, 136–153.

Argote, D., López-García, P., Torres-García, M., & Thrun, M. (2024). *Machine learning for archaeological applications in R*. Cambridge: Cambridge University Press.

Argote Espino, D., Solé, J., López García, P., & Sterpone, O. (2012). Obsidian sub-source identification in the Sierra de Pachuca and Otumba volcanic regions, Central Mexico, by ICP-MS and DBSCAN statistical analysis. *Geoarchaeology*, *27*, 48–62.

Bagus, A. & Pramana, S. (2016). *advclust: Object oriented advanced clustering, Version 0.4*. https://rdrr.io/rforge/advclust/.

Banfield, J. & Raftery, A. (1993). Model-based Gaussian and non-Gaussian clustering. *Biometrics*, *49*(*3*), 803–821.

Baudry, J., Raftery, A., Celeux, G., Lo, K., & Gottardo, R. (2010). Combining mixture components for clustering. *Journal of Computational and Graphical Statistics*, *9*(*2*), 332–353.

Baxter, M. (2001). Statistical modelling of artefact compositional data. *Archaeometry*, *43*(*1*), 131–147.

Baxter, M. (2015). *Notes on quantitative archaeology and R*. www.researchgate.net/publication/277931925_Notes_on_Quantitative_Archaeology_and_R.

Baxter, M. & Buck, C. (2000). Data handling and statistical analysis. In E. S. Ciliberto & G. Spoto (eds.), *Modern analytical methods in art and archaeology* (pp. 681–746). New York: Wiley-Interscience.

Baxter, M. & Cool, H. (2016). *Basic statistical graphics for archaeology with R: Life beyond Excel*. Nottingham: Barbican Research Associates and Nottingham Trent University.

Baxter, M., Beardah, C., Cool, H., & Jackson, C. (2003). Compositional data analysis in archaeometry. *CoDaWork03: Compositional Data Analysis Workshop*. Girona, Spain: Universitat de Girona. https://ima.udg.es/Activitats/CoDaWork03/paper_baxter_Beardah1.pdf.

Baxter, M., Beardah, C., Cool, H., & Jackson, C. (2005). Further studies in the compositional variability of colourless Romano-British vessel glass. *Archaeometry, 47(1)*, 47–68.

Baxter, M. & Jackson, C. (2001). Variable selection in artefact compositional studies. *Archaeometry, 43(2)*, 253–268.

Ben Dor, Y., Finkel, M., & Ben-Yosef, E. (2023). A probabilistic approach to provenance studies using whole object elemental composition: Chert (flint) as a case study. *Journal of Archaeological Science, 153*, 105767.

Ben-Gal, I. (2005). Outlier detection. In O. Maimon & L. Rokach (eds.), *Data mining and knowledge discovery handbook: A complete guide for practitioners and researchers* (pp. 131–146). New York: Springer.

Biernacki, C., Marbac, M., & Vandewalle, V. (2021). Gaussian-based visualization of Gaussian and non-Gaussian model-based clustering. *Journal of Classification, 38*, 129–157.

Bouveyron, C., Celeux, G., Murphy, T., & Raftery, A. (2019). *Model-based clustering and classification for data science with applications in R*. Cambridge Series in Statistical and Probabilistic Mathematics. Cambridge: Cambridge University Press.

Brock, G., Pihur, V., Datta, S., & Datta, S. (2008). clValid: An R package for cluster validation. *Journal of Statistical Software, 25(4)*, 1–22.

Carr, S. (2015). Geochemical characterization of obsidian subsources in Highland Guatemala. Unpublished BA thesis. Pennsylvania: Pennsylvania State University.

Cebeci, Z. (2020). fcvalid: An R package for internal validation of probabilistic and possibilistic clustering. *Sakarya University Journal of Computer and Information Sciences, 3(1)*, 11–27.

Celeux, G. & Govaert, G. (1995). Gaussian parsimonious clustering models. *Pattern Recognition, 28(5)*, 781–793.

References

Charrad, M., Ghazzali, N., Boiteau, V., & Niknafs, A. (2014). NbClust: An R package for determining the relevant number of clusters in a data set. *Journal of Statistical Software*, *61*(6), 1–36.

Cobean, R. (2002). *A world of obsidian: The mining and trade of a volcanic glass in ancient Mexico*. Mexico: INAH and Pittsburgh University.

Craig, N., Speakman, R., Popelka-Filcoff, R., Glascock, M., Robertson, J., Shackley, M., & Aldenderfer, M. (2007). Comparison of XRF and PXRF for analysis of archaeological obsidian from southern Perú. *Journal of Archaeological Science*, *34*(12), 2012–2024.

Cribbin, L. (2008). upclass: R package for performing updated classification rules. Unpublished MSc thesis. Dublin: University College Dublin.

Dagnino, J. (2014). Muestras, variabilidad y error. *Revista Chilena de Anestesia*, *43*(2), 100–103.

Dang, U., Gallaugher, M., Browne, R., & McNicholas, P. (2019). Model-based clustering and classification using mixtures of multivariate skewed power exponential distributions. *Journal of Classification*, *40*, 145–167.

Dempster, A., Laird, N., & Rubin, D. (1977). Maximum likelihood from incomplete data via the EM algorithm. *Journal of the Royal Statistical Society: Series B (Methodological)*, *39*(1), 1–22.

Desgraupes, B. (2018). *Package 'clusterCrit': Clustering indices*. https://CRAN.Rproject.org/package=clusterCrit.

Dolan, S. (2016). Black rocks in the borderlands: Obsidian procurement in southwestern New Mexico and northwestern Chihuahua, Mexico, AD 1000 to 1450. PhD dissertation. Oklahoma: University of Oklahoma Graduate College.

Dolan, S., Whalen, M., Minnis, P., & Shackley, M. (2017). Obsidian in the Casas Grandes world: Procurement, exchange, and interaction in Chihuahua, Mexico, CE 1200–1450. *Journal of Archaeological Science: Reports*, *11*, 555–567.

Duda, R., Hart, P., & Stork, D. (2001). *Pattern classification*. New York: John Wiley & Sons.

Egozcue, J. & Pawlowsky-Glahn, V. (2011). Análisis composicional de datos en ciencias geoambientales. *Boletín Geológico y Minero*, *122*(4), 439–452.

Egozcue, J., Pawlowsky-Glahn, V., Mateu-Figueras, G., & Barceló-Vidal, C. (2003). Isometric logratio transformations for compositional data analysis. *Mathematical Geology*, *35*(3), 279–300.

Etherington, T. (2019). Mahalanobis distances and ecological niche modelling: Correcting a chi-squared probability error. *PeerJ*, *7*, e6678.

Everitt, B., Landau, S., Leese, M., & Stahl, D. (2011). *Cluster analysis*. Wiley Series in Probability and Statistics Vol. 848. Chichester: John Wiley & Sons.

Filzmoser, P., Hron, K., & Reimann, C. (2009). Principal component analysis for compositional data with outliers. *Environmetrics*, *20*(*6*), 621–632.

Filzmoser, P., Hron, K., & Reimann, C. (2012). Interpretation of multivariate outliers for compositional data. *Computers & Geosciences*, *39*, 77–85.

Fish, P., Fish, S., Whittlesey, S., Neff, H., Glascock, M., & Elam, M. (1992). An evaluation of the production and exchange of Tanque Verde red-on-brown in southern Arizona. In H. Neff (ed.), *Chemical characterization of ceramic pastes in archaeology* (pp. 62–68). Madison: Prehistory Press.

Fisher, R. (1936). The use of multiple measurements in taxonomic problems. *Annals of Eugenics*, *7*(*2*), 179–188.

Fop, M. & Murphy, T. (2018). Variable selection methods for model-based clustering. *Statistics Surveys*, *12*, 18–65.

Fowlkes, E. & Mallows, C. (1983). A method for comparing two hierarchical clusterings. *Journal of the American Statistical Association*, *78*(*383*), 553–569.

Fraley, C. & Raftery, A. (1998). How many clusters? Which clustering method? Answers via model-based cluster analysis. *The Computer Journal*, *41*(*8*), 578–588.

Fraley, C., Raftery, A., Murphy, T., & Scrucca, L. (2012). *mclust version 4 for R: Normal mixture modeling for model-based clustering, classification, and density estimation*. Technical Report no. 597. Washington: Department of Statistics, University of Washington.

García-Heras, M., Blackman, J., Ruiz, M., & Bishop, R. (2001). Assessing ceramic compositional data: A comparison of total reflexion X-ray fluorescence and instrumental neutron activation analysis on late Iron Age Spanish Celtiberian ceramics. *Archaeometry*, *43*(*3*), 325–347.

Glascock, M. D. (1992). Characterization of archaeological ceramics at MURR by neutron activation analysis and multivariate statistics. In H. Neff (ed.), *Chemical characterization of ceramic pastes in archaeology* (pp. 11–26). Madison: Prehistory Press.

Glascock, M. D. (2002). Obsidian provenance research in the Americas. *Accounts of Chemical Research*, *35*(*8*), 611–617.

Glascock, M. D. (2011). Comparison and contrast between XRF and NAA: Used for characterization of obsidian sources in Central Mexico. In M. S. Shackley (ed.), *X-ray fluorescence spectrometry (XRF) in geoarchaeology* (pp. 161–192). New York: Springer.

Glascock, M. D. (2021). *MURRAP user guide*. https://archaeometry.missouri.edu/downloads/MURRAP_User_Guide.pdf.

Glascock, M. D. (2022). *GAUSS runtime download*. https://archaeometry.missouri.edu/gauss.html.

Glascock, M. D., Braswell, G., & Cobean, R. (1998). A systematic approach to obsidian source characterization. In M. S. Shackley (ed.), *Archaeological obsidian studies* (pp. 15–65). Boston: Springer.

Glascock, M. D., Weigand, P., Esparza López, R., Ohnersorgen, M., Garduño Ambriz, M., Mountjoy, J. & Darling, J. (2010). Geochemical characterisation of obsidian in Western Mexico: The sources in Jalisco, Nayarit, and Zacatecas. In Y. Kuzmin & M. D. Glascock, *Crossing the straits: Prehistoric obsidian source exploitation in the North Pacific Rim* (pp. 201–218). Oxford: Archaeopress.

Gordon, A. (1998). Cluster validation. In C. Hayashi, N. Ohsumi, K. Yajima, Y. Tanaka, H. Bock, & Y. Bada, *Data science, classification, and related methods* (pp. 22–39). Tokyo: Springer Tokyo.

Greenacre, M. (2017). *Towards a pragmatic approach to compositional data analysis*. Economics Working Paper Series, Working Paper no. 1554. Barcelona: Universitat Pompeu Fabra.

Haferlach, T., Kohlmann, A., Wieczorek, L., Basso, G., Te Kronnie, G., Béné, M.-C., De Vos, J., Hernández, J. M., Hofmann, W. K., Mills, K. I., Gilkes, A., Chiaretti, S., Shurtleff, S.A., Kipps, T. J., Rassenti, L. Z., Yeoh, A. E., Papenhausen, P. R., Liu, W. M., Williams, P. M., & Foà, R. (2010). Clinical utility of microarray-based gene expression profiling in the diagnosis and subclassification of leukemia: Report from the International Microarray Innovations in Leukemia Study Group. *Journal of Clinical Oncology*, *28*(*15*), 2529–2537.

Hall, M. (2004). Pottery production during the Late Jomon period: Insights from the chemical analyses of Kasori B pottery. *Journal of Archaeological Science*, *31*(*10*), 1439–1450.

Hall, M. & Minyaev, S. (2002). Chemical analyses of Xiong-Nu pottery: A preliminary study of exchange and trade on the inner Asian steppes. *Journal of Archaeological Science*, *29*(*2*), 135–144.

Handl, J., Knowles, J., & Kell, D. (2005). Computational cluster validation in post-genomic data analysis. *Bioinformatics*, *21*(*15*), 3201–3212.

Harbottle, G. (1976). Neutron activation analysis in archaeology. *Radiochemistry*, *3*, 33–72.

Harry, K. (1997). Ceramic production, distribution, and consumption in two Classic period Hohokam communities. Unpublished PhD thesis. Tucson, AZ: University of Arizona.

Harry, K., Fish, P., & Fish, S. (2002). Ceramic production and distribution in two classic period Hohokam communities. In D. Glowacki & H. Neff, *Ceramic production and circulation in the greater Southwest: Source determination by INAA and complementary mineralogical investigations* (pp. 99–109). Los Angeles: The Cotsen Institute of Archaeology, UCLA.

Hawkins, D. (1980). *Identification of outliers*. London: Chapman and Hall.

Heller, K. (2007). Efficient Bayesian methods for clustering. Unpublished PhD thesis. London, UK: University College London.

Hubert, M. & Van der Veeken, S. (2008). Outlier detection for skewed data. *Journal of Chemometrics, 22*(3–4), 235–246.

Hubert, M., Rousseeuw, P., & Vanden Branden, K. (2005). ROBPCA: A new approach to robust principal component analysis. *Technometrics, 47*(1), 64–79.

Iñañez, J., Speakman, R., Buxeda-i-Garrigós, J., & Glascock, M. D. (2009). Chemical characterization of tin-lead glazed pottery from the Iberian Peninsula and the Canary Islands: Initial steps toward a better understanding of Spanish colonial pottery in the Americas. *Archaeometry, 51*(4), 546–567.

Italiano, F., Correale, A., Di Bella, M., Martin, F., Martinelli, M., Sabatino, G., & Spatafora, F. (2018). The Neolithic obsidian artifacts from Roccapalumba (Palermo, Italy): First characterization and provenance determination. *Mediterranean Archaeology and Archaeometry, 18*(3), 151–167.

Jain, A. & Dubes, R. (1988). *Algorithms for clustering data*. Upper Saddle River, NJ: Prentice-Hall.

Kaufman, L. & Rousseeuw, P. (2005). *Finding groups in data: An introduction to cluster analysis*. Hoboken: Wiley.

Krijthe, J. H. (2017). RSSL: Semi-supervised learning in R. In B. Kerautret, M. Colom, & P. Monasse (eds.), *Reproducible research in pattern recognition. RRPR 2016* (pp. 104–115). Cham: Springer.

Langrognet, F., Lebret, R., Poli, C., Lovleff, S., & Auder, B. (2025). *Package 'Rmixmod' version 2.1.10: Classification with mixture modelling*. https://cloud.r-project.org/web/packages/Rmixmod/Rmixmod.pdf.

Lebret, R., Lovleff, S., Langrognet, F., Biernacki, C., Celeux, G., & Govaert, G. (2015). Rmixmod: The R package of the model-based unsupervised, supervised, and semi-supervised classification Mixmod library. *Journal of Statistical Software, 67*(6), 1–29.

Lerdo de Tejada Pavón, M. (2014). Estimación de datos faltantes con el Algoritmo EM. Unpublished thesis. Mexico: Universidad Nacional Autónoma de México.

López-García, P., Argote, D., & Thrun, M. (2020). Projection-based classification of chemical groups for provenance analysis of archaeological materials. *IEEE Access, 8*, 152439–152451.

López-García, P., Argote, D., Torres-García, M., & Thrun, M. (2024). *Knowledge discovery from archaeological materials*. Cambridge: Cambridge University Press.

López-García, P., García-Gómez, V., Acosta-Ochoa, G., & Argote, D. (2024). Semi-supervised classification to determine the provenance of archaeological obsidian samples. *Archaeometry*, *66*(*1*), 142–159.

Maechler, M. (2023). *CRAN task view: Robust statistical methods*. Version 2023-07-01. https://CRAN.R-project.org/view=Robust.

Maechler, M., Rousseeuw, P., Struyf, A., Hubert, M., & Hornik, K. (2024). *Cluster: Cluster analysis basics and extensions*. R package version 2.1.8. https://CRAN.R-project.org/package=cluster.

Marbac, M. & Sedki, M. (2017). Variable selection for model-based clustering using the integrated complete-data likelihood. *Statistics and Computing*, *27*(*4*), 1049–1063.

Martín-Fernández, J., Barceló-Vidal, C., & Pawlowsky-Glahn, V. (2003). Dealing with zeros and missing values in compositional data sets using nonparametric imputation. *Mathematical Geology*, *35*, 253–278.

Martín-Fernández, J., Buxeda i Garrigós, J., & Pawlowsky-Glahn, V. (2015). Logratio analysis in archaeometry: Principles and methods. In J. Barcelo & I. Bogdanovic (eds.), *Mathematics and archaeology* (pp. 178–189). Boca Raton: CRC Press.

Mateu-Figueras, G., Martín-Fernández, J., Pawlowsky-Glahn, V., & Barceló-Vidal, C. (2003). El problema del análisis estadístico de datos composicionales. *27° Congreso Nacional de Estadística e Investigación Operativa* (pp. 480–488). Lleida, Spain: Sociedad Española de Estadística e Investigación Operativa.

Maugis, C., Celeux, G., & Martin-Magniette, M. (2009a). Variable selection for clustering with Gaussian mixture models. *Biometrics*, *65*(*3*), 701–709.

Maugis, C., Celeux, G., & Martin-Magniette, M. (2009b). Variable selection in model-based clustering: A general variable role modeling. *Computational Statistics & Data Analysis*, *53*(*11*), 3872–3882.

McLachlan, G. & Peel, D. (2000). *Finite mixture models*. New York: Wiley.

Mendelsohn, R. (2018). Obsidian sourcing and dynamic trade patterns at Izapa, Chiapas, Mexico: 100 BCE–400 CE. *Journal of Archaeological Science: Reports*, *20*, 634–646.

Millhauser, J., Fargher, L., Heredia Espinoza, V., & Blanton, R. (2015). The geopolitics of obsidian supply in Postclassic Tlaxcallan: A portable X-ray fluorescence study. *Journal of Archaeological Science*, *58*, 133–146.

Millhauser, J., Rodríguez-Alegría, E., & Glascock, M. (2011). Testing the accuracy of portable X-ray fluorescence to study Aztec and Colonial obsidian supply at Xaltocan, Mexico. *Journal of Archaeological Science*, *38*(*11*), 3141–3152.

Milligan, G. & Cooper, M. (1988). A study of standardization of variables in cluster analysis. *Journal of Classification*, *5*, 181–204.

Moholy-Nagy, H., Meierhoff, J., Golitko, M., & Kestle, C. (2013). An analysis of pXRF obsidian source attributions from Tikal, Guatemala. *Latin American Antiquity*, *24(1)*, 72–97.

Murphy, T., Dean, N., & Raftery, A. (2010). Variable selection and updating in model-based discriminant analysis for high dimensional data with food authenticity applications. *The Annals of Applied Statistics*, *4(1)*, 396–421.

Neff, H. (1992). *Chemical characterization of ceramic pastes in archaeology.* Monographs in World Archaeology, vol. 7. Madison, WI: Prehistory Press.

Palarea-Albaladejo, J. & Martín-Fernández, J. (2015). zCompositions – R package for multivariate imputation of left-censored data under a compositional approach. *Chemometrics and Intelligent Laboratory Systems*, *143*, 85–96.

Pawlowsky-Glahn, V. & Buccianti, A. (2011). *Compositional data analysis: Theory and applications.* Chichester, UK: Wiley.

Pawlowsky-Glahn, V. & Egozcue, J. (2006). Compositional data and their analysis: An introduction. In A. Buccianti, G. Mateu-Figueras, & V. Pawlowsky-Glahn (eds.), *Compositional data analysis in the geosciences: From theory to practice* (pp. 1–10). Special Publication, vol. 264. London: Geological Society.

Pawlowsky-Glahn, V., Egozcue, J., & Tolosana-Delgado, J. (2007). *Lecture notes on compositional data analysis.* http://diobma.udg.edu/handle/10256/297/.

Pierce, D. (2015). Visual and geochemical analyses of obsidian source use at San Felipe Aztatán, Mexico. *Journal of Anthropological Archaeology*, *40*, 266–279.

R Core Team. (2020). *R: A language and environment for statistical computing.* https://cran.r-project.org/doc/manuals/r-release/fullrefman.pdf.

Raftery, A. & Dean, N. (2006). Variable selection for model-based clustering. *Journal of the American Statistical Association*, *101(473)*, 168–178.

Reimann, C., Filzmoser, P., & Garrett, R. (2002). Factor analysis applied to regional geochemical data: Problems and possibilities. *Applied Geochemistry*, *17(3)*, 185–206.

Rousseeuw, P. (1987). Silhouettes: A graphical aid to the interpretation and validation of cluster analysis. *Journal of Computational and Applied Mathematics*, *20*, 53–65.

Russell, N., Cribbin, L., & Murphy, T. (2013). *upclass-package: Updated classification methods using unlabeled data.* Version 2.0. https://rdrr.io/cran/upclass/man/upclass-package.html.

Salem, N. & Hussein, S. (2019). Data dimensional reduction and principal components analysis. *Procedia Computer Science*, *163*, 292–299.

Scrucca, L. & Raftery, A. (2018). clustvarsel: A package implementing variable selection for Gaussian model-based clustering in R. *Journal of Statistical Software*, *84(1)*, 1–28.

Sedki, M., Celeux, G., & Maugis, C. (2014). *SelvarMix: A R package for variable selection in model-based clustering and discriminant analysis with a regularization approach*. Research report no. hal-01053784. Retrieved from: https://hal.inria.fr/hal-01053784.

Sedki, M., Celeux, G., & Maugis-Rabusseau, C. (2017). *Package 'SelvarMix': Regularization for variable selection in model-based clustering and discriminant analysis*. https://CRAN.R-project.org/package=SelvarMix.

Shackley, M. S. (2005). *Obsidian: Geology and archaeology in the North American Southwest*. Tucson, AZ: University of Arizona Press.

Smith, M., Burke, A., Hare, T., & Glascock, M. (2007). Sources of imported obsidian at Postclassic sites in the Yautepec Valley, Morelos: A characterization study using XRF and INAA. *Latin American Antiquity*, *18(4)*, 429–450.

Thrun, M. (2018). *Projection-based clustering through self-organization and swarm intelligence: Combining cluster analysis with the visualization of high-dimensional data*. Heidelberg: Springer Vieweg.

Thrun, M. C. (2025). *Package: DatabionicSwarm (via r-universe): Swarm intelligence for self-organized clustering*. https://cran.r-universe.dev/DatabionicSwarm/DatabionicSwarm.pdf.

Thrun, M. C. & Ultsch, A. (2018). Effects of the payout system of income taxes to municipalities in Germany. *12th Professor Aleksander Zelias International Conference on Modelling and Forecasting of Socio-Economic Phenomena, vol. 1* (pp. 533–542). Zakopane, Poland: GfKl, Data Science Society.

Thrun, M. C. & Ultsch, A. (2021). Swarm intelligence for self-organized clustering. *Artificial Intelligence*, *290*, 103237.

Thrun, M. C., Pape, F., Hansen-Goos, O., & Ultsch, A. (2025, 01 26). *DataVisualizations: Visualizations of high-dimensional data*. https://CRAN.R-project.org/package=DataVisualizations.

Tykot, R. (2016). Using non-destructive portable X-ray fluorescence spectrometers on stone, ceramics, metals, and other materials in museums: Advantages and limitations. *Applied Spectroscopy*, *70(1)*, 42–56.

Ultsch, A. (1995). Self organizing neural networks perform different from statistical k-means clustering. *Proceedings of the Society for Information and Classification (GFKL)* (pp. 1–13). Basel, Switzerland.

Ultsch, A. & Thrun, M. C. (2017). Credible visualizations for planar projections. *Proceedings of the 12th International Workshop on Self-Organizing*

Maps and Learning Vector Quantization, Clustering and Data Visualization (WSOM 2017) (pp. 256–260). Nancy, France: IEEE.

van Buuren, S. & Groothuis-Oudshoorn, K. (2011). mice: Multivariate imputation by chained equations in R. *Journal of Statistical Software, 45*(3), 1–67.

van den Boogaart, K. & Tolosana-Delgado, R. (2013). *Analyzing compositional data with R.* London: Springer.

van den Boogaart, K., Tolosana-Delgado, R., & Bren, M. (2023). *Package 'compositions' versión 2.0–6: Compositional data analysis.* https://cran.r-project.org/web/packages/compositions/.

Varmuza, K. & Filzmoser, P. (2009). *Introduction to multivariate statistical analysis in chemometrics.* Boca Raton, FL: CRC Press.

Waite, D. (2020). Household economies and socioeconomic integration: An analysis of obsidian artifacts from Coba, Quintana Roo and Yaxuna, Yucatan, Mexico. MA thesis. Orlando, FL: University of Central Florida.

Wang, S. & Zhu, J. (2008). Variable selection for model-based high-dimensional clustering and its application to microarray data. *Biometrics, 64*(2), 440–448.

Wehrens, R. (2011). *Chemometrics with R: Multivariate data analysis in the natural and life sciences.* Berlin: Springer-Verlag.

Weigand, P., Harbottle, G., & Sayre, E. (1977). Turquoise sources and source analysis: Mesoamerica and the Southwestern U.S.A. In T. Earle & J. Ericson (eds.), *Exchange systems in prehistory* (pp. 15–34). New York: Academic Press.

Wilkinson, L. & Friendly, M. (2009). The history of the cluster heat map. *The American Statistician, 63*(2), 179–184.

Xie, B., Pan, W., & Shen, X. (2008). Penalized model-based clustering with cluster-specific diagonal covariance matrices and grouped variables. *Electronic Journal of Statistics, 2,* 168–212.

Xu, R. & Wunsch, D. (2005). Survey of clustering algorithms. *IEEE Transactions on Neural Networks, 16*(3), 645–678.

Zaki, M. & Meira, W. (2014). *Data mining and analysis: Fundamental concepts and algorithms.* New York: Cambridge University Press.

Zhu, X. & Goldberg, A. (2009). *Introduction to semi-supervised learning.* Synthesis Lectures on Artificial Intelligence and Machine Learning, no. 6. Cham: Springer.

Cambridge Elements =

Current Archaeological Tools and Techniques

Hans Barnard
Cotsen Institute of Archaeology

Hans Barnard was associate adjunct professor in the Department of Near Eastern Languages and Cultures as well as associate researcher at the Cotsen Institute of Archaeology, both at the University of California, Los Angeles. He currently works at the Roman site of Industria in northern Italy and previously participated in archaeological projects in Armenia, Chile, Egypt, Ethiopia, Italy, Iceland, Panama, Peru, Sudan, Syria, Tunisia, and Yemen. This is reflected in the seven books and more than 100 articles and chapters to which he contributed.

Willeke Wendrich
Polytechnic University of Turin

Willeke Wendrich is Professor of Cultural Heritage and Digital Humanities at the Politecnico di Torino (Turin, Italy). Until 2023 she was Professor of Egyptian Archaeology and Digital Humanities at the University of California, Los Angeles, and the first holder of the Joan Silsbee Chair in African Cultural Archaeology. Between 2015 and 2023 she was Director of the Cotsen Institute of Archaeology, with which she remains affiliated. She managed archaeological projects in Egypt, Ethiopia, Italy, and Yemen, and is on the board of the International Association of Egyptologists, Museo Egizio (Turin, Italy), the Institute for Field Research, and the online UCLA Encyclopedia of Egyptology.

About the Series

Cambridge University Press and the Cotsen Institute of Archaeology at UCLA collaborate on this series of Elements, which aims to facilitate deployment of specific techniques by archaeologists in the field and in the laboratory. It provides readers with a basic understanding of selected techniques, followed by clear instructions how to implement them, or how to collect samples to be analyzed by a third party, and how to approach interpretation of the results.

Cambridge Elements

Current Archaeological Tools and Techniques

Elements in the Series

Archaeological Mapping and Planning
Hans Barnard

Mobile Landscapes and Their Enduring Places
Bruno David, Jean-Jacques Delannoy and Jessie Birkett-Rees

Cultural Burning
Bruno David, Michael-Shawn Fletcher, Simon Connor, Virginia Ruth Pullin, Jessie Birkett-Rees, Jean-Jacques Delannoy, Michela Mariani, Anthony Romano and S. Yoshi Maezumi

Knowledge Discovery from Archaeological Materials
Pedro A. López-García, Denisse L. Argote, Manuel A. Torres-García and Michael C. Thrun

Machine Learning for Archaeological Applications in R
Denisse L. Argote, Pedro A. López-García, Manuel A. Torres-García and Michael C. Thrun

Worked Bone, Antler, Ivory, and Keratinous Materials
Adam DiBattista

Infrared Spectroscopy of Archaeological Sediments
Michael B. Toffolo

Retrospective and Prospective for Scientific Provenance Studies in Archaeology
A.M. Pollard

Archaeological Wood and Woodworking
Caroline Arbuckle MacLeod

Bioarchaeology of Infants and Children
L. Creighton Avery

Ceramic Analysis: Laboratory Methods
Irmgard Hein, Mustafa Kibaroğlu, Michaela Schauer, Anno Hein, Georgios Polymeris, Judit Molera, Trinitat Pradell

Determining Provenance from Compositional Data
Pedro A. López-García and Denisse L. Argote

A full series listing is available at: www.cambridge.org/EATT